PRAIRIE SMOKE

MELVIN R. GILMORE

ILLUSTRATED BY
LOUIS SCHELLBACH

With a New Introduction
by Roger L. Welsch

MINNESOTA HISTORICAL SOCIETY PRESS
ST. PAUL • 1987

9214966

Borealis Books are high-quality paperback reprints of books chosen by the Minnesota Historical Society Press for their importance as enduring historical sources and their value as enjoyable accounts of life in the Upper Midwest.

MINNESOTA HISTORICAL SOCIETY PRESS, St. Paul 55101
First published 1929 by Columbia University Press
New material copyright © 1987 by the Minnesota Historical Society

International Standard Book Number 0-87351-207-3
Manufactured in the United States of America

10 9 8 7 6 5 4 3 2 1

Library of Congress Cataloging-in-Publication Data
Gilmore, Melvin R. (Melvin Randolf), 1868–1940
Prairie smoke.
(Borealis)
Reprint. Originally published: New York : Columbia University Press, 1929.
"Works by Melvin R. Gilmore": p.
Includes index.
1. Indians of North America—Great Plains—Legends.
2. Indians of North America—Great Plains—Social life
and customs. I. Title.
E78.G73G54   1987   398.2'08997078   86–31205
ISBN 0-87351-207-3 (pbk.)

DEDICATION

To the Real Pioneers of the Great Plains: to those whose questing spirit first sought out the wonders and the beauties of this land — its vast reaches, league upon league, of grassland, verdant in springtime, sere and red and brown in autumn, its inviting valleys and forbidding buttes; to those whose moccasined feet made the first human footprints upon the turf of these prairies and upon the sands of these river margins; whose self-reliance made them the first to breast the current of these streams; whose humble footpaths over the land have now become the transcontinental highways of the world's travel and trade; to those who first slaked thirst at these cool, clear water springs; whose hunger was first satisfied by the fruits of this land; and who, in eating and in drinking, devoutly gave thanks to our tender Mother Earth for her bounties, receiving them gratefully as sacred gifts to be used prudently and enjoyed thankfully, and never to be wasted; who knew and loved this land in all its spacious extent, east to west and south to north; who reverenced its sacred places, the holy water springs, the grand and silent hills, the mysterious caves, the eerie precipices — all places where their fathers had with prayer and fasting sought and obtained the favor of the gods, and where the gods had granted revelations and given wisdom; to those whose eyes first beheld this land in its virgin beauty, fresh and joyous, unscarred and unspoiled, clean and wholesome, animated with exuberance of life of many species of both plant and animal in wonderful balance and adjustment, spontaneously replenished; and who held it sacrilege to violate or in any way endanger that delicate balance of nature; to those first inhabitants of this land which we now inhabit — that something of their appreciation, of their love and reverence for the land and its native life, something of their respect for its sacred places and holy associations, something of their sense of its charm, its beauty and wonder, may come to us, that we may the more worthily occupy and more sympathetically enjoy our tenure of this land.

CONTENTS

CONTENTS

CONTENTS

INTRODUCTION TO THE REPRINT EDITION

Prairie Smoke is one of those rare works in which an author successfully combines the solid investigative work of a practicing scientist with the unabashed affection the Romantic inevitably holds for American Indians. And that is not surprising, because Melvin Gilmore's life was a remarkable exercise in combining disparate tastes and interests into new studies — studies that go in quite different directions well beyond their original disciplines. While many of his findings may seem basic today, in his time they represented pioneering ventures, fresh research in unexplored cultural and geographical zones.

Gilmore was a professional ethnobotanist and a prolific writer. As the bibliography at the end of this volume demonstrates, he wrote on a wide variety of topics for a wide variety of popular and scientific periodicals.[1] His interests were diverse, but rather than compartmentalize them, keeping each separate from the others, he blended them, producing rich new understandings of the Plains and its peoples, new conclusions about scientific methodology and application. He applied rigorous, serious accuracy to recording oral data, thus providing us

[1] I am grateful to Alan R. Woolworth for his work in preparing the exhaustive bibliography that appears for the first time in this edition.

with authentic Indian lore. (This material had previously been used only by popular antiquarians who reworked it for the amusement, but rarely the enlightenment, of their readers.) Gilmore did not concentrate, as the botanist might, only on taxonomic lists, nor did he restrict himself, as the popular antiquarian might, to myths. By studying and publishing his work combining the two interests, he allowed his readers then and now to understand the very real and very fundamental relationship between those two fields: plants explain tales, and tales explain plants.

For his title, Gilmore selected an evocative image, one that would "recall lively recollections of both sight and scent." Indeed, the book *Prairie Smoke* is like the flower prairie smoke, which the author describes as producing a "nebulous appearance presented by a patch of the bluish blossoms upon a prairie hillside in early spring, while all other vegetation is still brown and dead. At such a time, with all their flowers tremulous in the spring wind, they appear to the view like a pulsing cloud of grayish-blue smoke hovering low over the ground" (page xxvii). Taken as a whole, Gilmore's short essays in this book — and, for that matter, in his life's work — take on an air that is at once ephemeral and yet undeniably real. When we read *Prairie Smoke,* we do not simply acquire an inventory of facts about the Plains and Plains Indian ethnology; we are given a new understanding of the essence of that culture in that geography.

Gilmore meant *Prairie Smoke* to be a popular book, written for the newcomer to Plains Indian culture or the young reader, and it was composed at a time when use of the English language was a good deal more flamboyant than is customary today. "Each of us carries with him the germs of happiness or of unhappiness," Gilmore wrote. "Those of unhappy disposition will be unhappy wherever they may be. Cheer is not in environment, but in the individual. One who is of a cheerful, understanding disposition will find interest and cheer wherever he may be. . . . So it is hoped that to each one who reads this little volume it may indeed be as a wisp of prairie smoke, bringing a real savor of the prairie and at least a slight realization of what the Prairie was before it was swept by the destructive Fires of Change" (page xxv, xxvii).

That sort of melodramatic prose must not obscure for the modern reader the fact that Gilmore was precisely this passionate about the Plains, its people, its plants, and animals. The language is not, therefore, an affectation. Moreover, the studied, literary form of his prose reflects to a useful degree the importance of eloquence in Plains Indian speech. Still today Plains Indians place a good deal of weight on oratorical skills; there is scarcely any Omaha or Sioux gathering where there is not a time set aside for speech making. The language used on such occasions is dramatic and poetic — not unlike Gilmore's.

Secondly, the reader should not dismiss Gilmore's role as a serious and respected scholar because of his florid language or because his book is directed toward a popular audience. Gilmore knew what he was writing about. His knowledge may not be as thorough as that of modern researchers because he was a pioneer in the field and lacked the bibliographic groundwork available to us now. But his careful observation and his acceptance by the Indian people with whom he worked give us, in *Prairie Smoke,* an important resource, regardless of its intended audience. It is true that *Prairie Smoke* does not have the clear focus the serious researcher looks for in a modern ethnology; it jumps from Omaha to Pawnee, from the prairie rose to tribal boundaries, from creation myths to trickster tales. But this arrangement is part of Gilmore's purpose, not the result of a dilettante's aimlessness. He mixed his field-collected materials together into a haze like that of the pasque flower because that was the way the stories, beliefs, plants, customs, and animals interacted and blended in the real world of the Indians he knew so well — and that is, after all, the way these things appear in normal conversation and life. Gilmore intended the book as an introductory text, an *hors d'oeuvre* that might lure the reader to more serious inquiry.

Moreover, in all of Gilmore's work there is a hint of the purposeful, directed, even polemic that burned most intensely in his life — his insistence that we more recent visitors to the Plains should respect the inherent nature of the landscape, learn to live within its historical-botanical-zoological matrix, and abandon our bankrupt European folklore, accepting that of the Indians who had obviously thrived here, nurtured, in part, by their folklore. He wanted us to cultivate plants that had for centuries proven their vitality here rather than introduce

new crops or wrench the Plains with devices like irrigation to make possible agriculture that is not immediately
suitable to the region. In short, rather than making the
Plains into a landscape compatible with our ideas of
what a landscape should be, we should, Gilmore tried to
convince us, adapt ourselves to fit what the Plains already
are.

Prairie Smoke is part of that polemic. The stories in
this collection give us a hint of how the Plains Indian saw
himself as an integral component of the world around
him — the animals, the plants, the hills, the wind —
rather than as a godlike manipulator of events or as a vic-
tim in a systemless mess of random coincidences, un-
likely notions which even the modern Plains Indian
views with bemusement. Gilmore, who had worked with
the Boy and Girl Scouts of America and was an honorary
member of the Council of Campfire Girls for greater
Iowa, hoped that young readers would be attracted to
the romance of Indian folklore, would come to understand the obvious utility of Plains ethnobotany, and
then would enter into the mutually beneficial interrela-
tionship between the Indians and the Plains. The shards
of nonmaterial artifacts that this book offers let us reso-
nate with the basic emotions and perceptions of the people of the Plains: "The gale of wind roared unceasingly;
the myriad millions of tiny snow particles ground upon
each other in the swirl of the storm, each infinitesimal
impact adding to the aggregate of reverberation of
sound, while the skin tents hummed like enormous
drums" (page 117), or "In smoking, Indians did not

seize the pipestem in the teeth. Such an act would be sacrilegious. The mouthpiece of the pipestem was gently presented to the lips and the breath was drawn through. By this inspiration the smoker united the mystery of the tobacco, the mystery of fire and the mystery of the breath of life" (page 208).

The mysticism in many of these essays is not a violation of the scientist's objectivity but an accurate reflection of the mysticism inherent in Plains Indian culture at Gilmore's time and yet today. Perhaps *Prairie Smoke* is a suitable balance for the modern, scientific archaeology that never once asks about the name of the woman who used this grinding stone, or whom the maker of this flint knife loved, or what the people of this lodge thought about when they looked into a clear winter sky.

Gilmore's work compares well with that of the ethnologists and ethnographers who preceded and followed him. "How Coyote Chief Was Punished" (pages 119–123), for example, is a typical Plains trickster tale in which Coyote is both clever and stupid, heroic and cowardly, animal, god, and man. Gilmore's rendition is similar to, but more readable than, the version published by James Owen Dorsey in *Cegiha Language* and later retranslated and republished in my *Omaha Tribal Myths and Trickster Tales*.[2] "An Omaha Ghost Story"

---

[2]Dorsey, *Cegiha Language* (Washington, D.C.: Department of the Interior, U.S. Geographical and Geological Survey, 1890); Welsch, *Omaha Tribal Myths and Trickster Tales* (Athens, Ohio: Ohio University Press, 1981).

(pages 67–70) is one I heard in almost the same form on the Omaha reservation forty years after the tale appeared in *Prairie Smoke*. It is almost impossible that the Omaha who told me the story were familiar with Gilmore. It seems more likely the Omaha and Gilmore were both familiar with the same narrative tradition.

As I read *Prairie Smoke* I find echoes of passages I have read in the works of John G. Neihardt, Alice C. Fletcher and Francis La Flesche, and Margaret Mead.[3] Again and again I am reminded of conversations I have had with Omaha and Sioux. The same things were said to me that had been said to Gilmore decades earlier — and then accurately recorded and reported in *Prairie Smoke*. Perhaps more important, this book includes the same sorts of information that Gilmore was publishing in his scientific works. The author did not reserve his scholarship for scholars alone.

Gilmore was born near Valley, Nebraska, in 1868 and grew up there as a farm boy. He taught school in nearby Elk City and attended normal school at Fremont, the closest place he could study and still be near his home. His interests in ethnology, science, and museum interpretation led him to develop exhibits at the Pan-

---

[3]John G. Neihardt, *Black Elk Speaks* (New York: W. Morrow and Company, 1932); Alice C. Fletcher and Francis La Flesche, *The Omaha Tribe*, Bureau of American Ethnology Report, 1905–06 (Washington, D.C.: Government Printing Office, 1911), 17–672; Margaret Mead, *The Changing Culture of an Indian Tribe* (New York: Columbia University Press, 1932).

American Exposition in Buffalo, New York, in 1901. He graduated from Cotner University in Bethany, Nebraska, in 1904 or 1905 and taught there from 1904 until 1911. He also pursued graduate work at the University of Nebraska during the years 1904 to 1914, studying under the charismatic botanist Charles E. Bessey (he earned his master's degree in 1909 and Ph.D. in 1914). From 1911 to 1916 he was also a fieldworker and exhibits and collections interpreter at the Nebraska State Historical Society.[4]

Gilmore continued with a distinguished career of publications and museum service as curator of the State Historical Society of North Dakota (1916–23), at the Museum of the American Indian in New York City (1923–28), and at the University of Michigan, Ann Arbor (1928–ca. 1937), where he established an ethnobotanical laboratory. From 1922, he was also on the teaching staffs of the American School of Wild Life Protection in McGregor, Iowa, and the Nature Training School at Gardner Lake, Connecticut. During these years, his work expanded to include study among the Arikara, Hidatsa, Mandan, Osage, Chippewa, and Onondaga cultures.

What lie hidden beneath these facts and dates, typical of academic biographies, are the growing interests that

---

[4]All of the material dealing with Gilmore's personal and academic life is taken from David L. Erickson, "Melvin Randolph Gilmore, Incipient Cultural Ecologist: A Biographic Analysis" (Master's thesis, University of Nebraska, Lincoln, 1971).

Gilmore developed in Plains Indians and botany, fields that had traditionally been thought of as very disparate sorts of pursuits. To the casual observer these studies may seem an unusual combination — folktales and weeds — but not to anyone who has worked seriously with any specific ecology and an ethnology native to it. This broad and comprehensive view enabled Gilmore to obtain and share with his readers information that no one else was collecting, perhaps that no one even could collect.

There is, I believe, a predictable progression of attitudes that develops within any sensitive person who spends time on a landscape as distinctive as the Plains or with a cultural group as attractive as the Plains Indians. First the observer is curious about and fascinated by what he sees; there is almost a bewilderment at what appears to be a denial of what was clearly fact before. What seemed to be a matter of human nature is suddenly and clearly no more than a matter of cultural learning. Concepts as fundamental as the nature of time and the value of property are swept away as the fieldworker discovers that what had seemed to be the "normal order" of things is simply a set of ideas taught by one's parents, and, what is worse, that these ideas can seem venal and petty in the face of another culture that languishes in a distinctly inferior position. What seemed right becomes wrong, and what seemed unthinkable becomes logical. When that happens to the anthropologist, folklorist, or even casual cultural traveler, that person has made the step of cross-identification that is crucial to substantive field work. Gilmore did that.

Then there is a period of sadness as the transcultural explorer worries about the injustice that the culture he is experiencing has suffered at the hands of the dominant, majority group — in our case, the imminent destruction of Plains Indian culture by the dominant Anglo-American one. Why, the observer asks, have others not seen and appreciated the beauty and nobility that is so obvious to him? And the observer now takes steps, usually small and perhaps even pathetic, to alleviate what he perceives as mistreatment.

Next the outsider comes to realize that in addition to struggling on behalf of this new advocacy, it is even more important to continue learning what the landscape and its peoples have to share; the only way the rest of the world is going to find a similar appreciation is to know the same sorts of things that have brought the observer to a new understanding. In my own case, I found that far from stealing too much from the Omaha, we had actually not stolen enough. Having taken land, game, and place names, we had left behind the most valuable of the treasures — the knowledge the Omaha still have of the Plains, its plants, its ways.

This, I believe, happened to Gilmore during his years growing up on the Nebraska farm, studying under Bessey, working at the Nebraska State Historical Society, and, most importantly, pursuing field work among Plains Indians. His burgeoning knowledge of the Plains and its people was drawing him inextricably into a love affair — not with each entity separately but with the two as part and parcel of the same eco-cultural complex. I can write so confidently of these undocumented, personal aspects of Gilmore's development because I went through precisely the same transitions, with the same landscape and the same people — the Omaha. In Gilmore's words I find an echo of my own feelings.

From 1905 to 1910 Gilmore studied among the Omaha on their reservation on the Missouri River north of Omaha, and these years were the most productive and formative of his life. In 1912 he expanded his field work to the Pine Ridge Reservation in South Dakota (that is, the Oglala Sioux) while continuing his work among the Omaha. In 1913 he spent time with the Pawnee, Teton Sioux, Ponca, Santee Sioux, Omaha, and Winnebago, funded by the state legislature of Nebraska. This was Gilmore's best year in the field, and, one should note, a demonstration of remarkably good sense by the legislature.

In 1914 and 1915 Gilmore continued his work with the Omaha and spent additional time with the Pawnee, now in part studying ethnozoology as well as ethnobotany. While in North Dakota he studied among the Arikara on the Fort Berthold Reservation. During his years in the East and in Michigan his heart remained on the Plains and among the Indians of the Plains. Sometime around 1937 he returned to his home, settling in Lincoln, Nebraska, where he died in 1940 after a long illness.

Melvin Gilmore was not an armchair Romantic who carried home his stories and customs where he could skewer them like butterflies in a collection. He expressed his affection for the Plains and its people with a vigorous activism on behalf of both. He urged the adoption and adaptation of native Plains plants for agricultural profit. Native maize, Sandhills wild rice, sand cherries, tipsin, buffalo berry, and ground beans, he argued, were already hardy and vigorous residents of the region; farmers needed only to understand how to grow and harvest them. There are many of us who believe that Gilmore's lesson will still have to be learned by the later generations of settlers, all the more difficult to do because we have delayed so long.

Perhaps we can also still learn something from Gilmore's intense regard for the Indian "botanists" with whom he worked. His remarkable research successes resulted in large part from that regard: "I find myself able to disarm their suspicion and overcome their reticence and enter into conversation with them on things they never discuss with a white man. Not encountering any supercilious curiosity in my attitude in conversation, and being induced by the knowledge of Indian matters they find me already possessed of they come almost unconsciously to talk of other things with me as with another Indian, thus adding to my information[.] I make it a painless process for them, which is the only practicable process of extraction of information from them, for Indians are very sensitive."[5]

This edition of *Prairie Smoke* was published in 1929,

[5]Gilmore to Clarence Sumner Paine, November 28, 1913, cited in Erickson, 72–73.

two previous, slimmer versions having appeared in 1921 and 1922 (Bismarck Tribune Press: Bismarck, North Dakota). While *Prairie Smoke* is first of all an entertaining book of Plains Indian culture, it is also a collection solidly based in authentic Plains Indian lore as collected in person, in the field, by a serious, objective, and academically trained scientist. While it was intended by Gilmore as a popular and introductory text, mature and even anthropologically sophisticated readers will find it engaging and instructive, especially if we keep in mind the intent Melvin Gilmore expressed in his Dedication, "that something of [the Indians'] appreciation, of their love and reverence for the land and its native life, something of their respect for its sacred places and holy associations, something of their sense of its charm, its beauty and wonder, may come to us, that we may the more worthily occupy and more sympathetically enjoy our tenure of this land."

— *Roger Welsch*

PREFACE

Many persons are ever seeking outside of themselves and in some distant place or time for interest and cheer. They are always discontented and complaining. They fancy if they were but in some other place or other circumstances they would be happy. But this is a vain fancy. Each of us carries with him the germs of happiness or of unhappiness. Those of unhappy disposition will be unhappy wherever they may be. Cheer is not in environment, but in the individual. One who is of a cheerful, understanding disposition will find interest and cheer wherever he may be.

Robert Louis Stevenson well said, "The world is so full of a number of things, I think we should all be as happy as kings." When there are so many interesting things in the world, so many in any given place, so many more than one can ever fully know or enjoy in the short span of human lifetime, how can one ever be overtaken by dullness? If dullness seem to enfold us, be sure is is we that are dull; it is because our minds are lazy and our eyes unseeing. There is enough of interest about us, wherever we may be, to engage our attention if we open our eyes to it. If we have initiative and independence of mind, we shall find interest everywhere; but if we depend upon others, or neglect what is about us in desire for what is distant, we shall never be content. One greater than Robert Louis Stevenson said, "The kingdom of heaven is within you."

It is with the purpose of calling attention to some of the many fascinating, interesting things which we have all about us on the prairies and plains and in the hills and valleys of our own region, and perhaps in our own neighborhood, that this volume is produced. The myths which pertain to the hills, valleys, springs and streams in our own state and in our own neighborhood must be of interest to us when we look with our own eyes upon the actual places to which these myths pertain. And these myths of the country in which we live are at least equal in beauty and interest to the myths of the Greeks, and to the old Teutonic myths of Thor, Odin and Freya, or even to our own old British myths which we have from our Druidic ancestors. However beautiful and interesting in itself a native tree or flower or other plant may be, however engaging to the attention may be a native bird or beast, how much more so when we think of what this bird or beast or flower or tree has been in the lives of generations of our fellow men who have lived here and loved this land and its teeming native life long before we ever saw it.

So, it is with the purpose of directing the attention of our people to the wealth of lore, of legend and story and myth, and of wonder and beauty which lies all about us here if we but look and listen, that this little volume is presented.

The title of this book is suggested by one of the popular names of a flower which is the subject of one of the stories in this volume. This flower, the earliest to bloom in springtime over all the northern prairies, has a number of popular names, among which are "pasque flower," "gosling flower," and "prairie smoke." The latter name is suggested by the nebulous appearance presented by a patch of the bluish blossoms upon a prairie hillside in early spring, while all other vegetation is still brown and dead. At such a time, with all their flowers tremulous in the spring wind, they appear to the view like a pulsing cloud of grayish-blue smoke hovering low over the ground.

Besides the reference to this dearly loved prevernal flower, the term "prairie smoke" also connotes a number of other engaging conceptions. To one who has lived upon the prairie this term will recall lively recollections of both sight and scent. It will recall to the imagination memories of rolling billows of smoke which he has seen covering miles of advancing lines of prairie fire; he will see again in memory the tiny blue spirals of smoke showing where some solid particles still smoulder hours after the line of fire has passed on, leaving behind a vast blackened waste. It will recall to him also the rare, intangible blue haze which for days after such a fire lay like a veil over all the plain, and through which the sun appeared like a great red disk hanging in the sky, while the air was redolent with an indescribable tang. Again, it brings to mind the wisps of smoke which once curled upward in the quiet summer air from stovepipes projecting from the roofs of prairie sod houses, or which on snowy winter mornings hung above them like thin white scarfs against a vast background of blue overhanging a white world.

It will bring to mind also other days and other scenes

of this same prairie country, when wreaths of smoke issued from the domes of the hemispherical houses of villages of Mandans, Pawnees, or Omahas, upon the hills and river terraces, with their laboriously tilled cornfields and gardens in the fertile alluvial valleys near by. Or again it will recall the scene of an encampment of some of these people out upon the prairie on a buffalo hunt in quest of their meat supply. The encampment is a circle of conical tents, a circle of perhaps a half mile in diameter. Before each tent the evening fire is twinkling in the dusk upon the green of the prairie, one in a circle of friendly lights, each the center of a family group, while a few stars begin to twinkle in the blue of the sky above, and the sunset colors glow in the horizon.

Some or all of these sights and scents, and others also, will present themselves according to the experience of the one who comprehends the title "Prairie Smoke."

So it is hoped that to each one who reads this little volume it may indeed be as a wisp of prairie smoke, bringing a real savor of the prairie and at least a slight realization of what the Prairie was before it was swept by the destructive Fires of Change.

PRAIRIE SMOKE

MOTHER EARTH

THE PRAIRIE

To obtain even an approximate appreciation of the conditions of life as they presented themselves to the people of the nations which formerly occupied the region drained by the Missouri River and its tributaries, we must bring ourselves to see it as it was in its natural condition, void of all the countless changes and accessories which we have made here by our European culture and custom.

Imagine, then, a country of open prairie stretching away and away, beyond the range of vision, over hill, valley, and plain, the skyline unbroken by trees, except a fringe along the course of a stream. The aspect of this landscape in summer was that of a boundless sea of shining green, billowing under the prevailing south wind, darkened here and there by the swiftly marching shadows of clouds sailing high and white in the brilliant blue sky. Toward the end of summer the sun appears to have shed some of its luster upon the plain below, for it now shines with a paler light, while the ever-restless, rustling, whispering sea of grass waves in rolling billows of golden green, seeming to be forever flowing on before the south wind into the mysterious North, changing again into yellow and warm brown as autumn comes on.

Then it may happen some day that the whole aspect is suddenly changed. Fire has escaped in the sea of dry grass. To the windward the horizon is one long line of smoke, which, as it comes nearer, rolls up in black masses shot through with darting tongues of angry red flames leaping a hundred feet skyward, while the sound of the conflagration is like that of a rushing storm. Frightened animals are fleeing before it in terror for their lives, and birds are flying from the threatened destruction.

This scene passes, and now the whole visible earth is one vast stretch of coal-black, and the whole sky is a thick blue haze in which the sun seems to hang like a great red ball, while an unbroken silence pervades the land.

Then winter comes with days of leaden sky and blackened earth, succeeded by clear days when the snow-covered earth appears like a vast white bowl encrusted with frost-diamonds and inclosed by an overarching dome of most brilliant blue.

Again the season changes: warm airs blow from the south; soft showers fall; the sound of the first thunder wakens all Nature; the blackened earth appears once more, soon showing color from the pale green spears of tender young grass, and in a short time the form of Mother Earth is once more clothed in a mantle of shining green.

And now, as the biting winds of winter yield to the balmy breezes from the south, all the vernal flora is quickened into life and beauty. The modest blue violets appear in such profuse abundance that they seem like shreds of the sky wafted by the spring breezes over the land and drifted into every swale and ravine. On the upland the purple flowers of the buffalo pea show themselves; in sandy places of the Middle Great Plains the dainty lavender blue bonnets of the early windflower are trembling in the breeze. In the Northern Great Plains the snow is scarcely gone before the pasque flowers, first gladsome harbingers of the lovely hosts to follow, troop forth over the bleak hillsides—"very brave little flowers," the Cree Indians say, "which arrive while it is still so cold that they must come wearing their fur coats." This is in allusion to the furry appearance of the pasque flower.

And as the floral life manifests itself, all the native faunal life is also awakened to a renewed activity. Migratory birds are seen and heard flying northward by relays in hundreds of thousands. The course of the Missouri River marks upon the earth the chart by which they direct their northward flight toward their summer homing places. The Arkansas River, the Kansas, the Platte, the Niobrara and the White River are relay stations of their journey, and the countless V-shaped flocks coming northward in long lines wheel, circling down until tracts many acres in extent are whitened by the great numbers of snow geese, while the Canada geese in equal numbers darken other tracts; ducks in great numbers are swimming on all the ponds and quiet streams, and regiments and brigades of tall gray cranes are continually marching and countermarching on land or sailing like fleets of monoplanes far up in the clear blue, whence float down to earth the vibrant notes of their bugle calls as they travel on into the North. On the higher prairies at sunrise as the long rays of the red morning sun slant brightly across the land the booming, drum-like sound of hundreds of prairie chickens is heard at their assemblies, for at this season they dance the mating dance at the sunrise hour. Soon the meadow larks, "the birds of promise," appear, singing their songs of promise of good things for their friends, the human beings; and they set about the duties of housekeeping, building their lowly nests at the grass roots, and all about are scenes of brightness and sounds of gladness.

It was in such a country as this, then, that the people of the different native nations who were here before us lived and took joy from the good gifts of Mother Earth and from their own activities, and in all the beauty of this good land. And they loved this land for all its good gifts and for its beauty, and for these and for its mystery and grandeur they paid reverence.

THE WATER SPRING OF THE HOLY MAN

Long ago there was a village of people of the Dakota nation which was situated on the east side of the great river which they call the Muddy Water, but which white people call the Missouri River. The white people named it so from the Missouri nation of Indians on the lower course of this great river.

The village that I have mentioned was on the east side of the river, nearly opposite to the mouth of the Cannon Ball River. The people were happy in this village, for it was a pleasant place. There was plenty of wood for their fires, and there was an abundance of buffalo berries, wild plums, choke-cherries, June berries, wild grapes, wild raspberries and other fruit growing in the woods. Upon the high prairie there was much tipsin, whose roots are so good when cooked with meat or with dried green corn. Moreover, in the timber were many box elder trees, whose sap was made into sugar in early springtime. Not far away were some lakes where there were many wild ducks and geese and other waterfowl. The flesh and also the eggs of these birds were good food. Upon the prairie were herds of buffaloes and antelopes and elks, and in the timber along the river were many deer.

And below the hills, on the level ground of the river valley, there was fertile soil where they planted their fields of corn and beans and squashes. They also cultivated the great sunflowers, whose seeds are so good for food.

And the people loved this place, for besides all the good things to eat, and other comforts which it gave them, it was also pleasant to look upon. There was the mysterious river, coming down from the distant mountains away in the northwest and flowing on towards the lands of other nations of people in the southeast; its channel could be seen winding its gleaming way among the dark trees on its shores. Upon the prairie hills in early spring the courageous little pasque flowers appeared like a gray-blue cloud let down upon the hilltops, where they nodded their cheery greetings to the people who passed them. In the vales a little later were masses of deep-blue violets. Still later, the prairie was bright with the color and the air was sweet with the breath of the wild rose of the prairie. The cheery meadow lark, which the people call "the bird of promise," flitted here and there and called his greetings and promised good things to his friends, the Dakota people.

And through the procession of the seasons there were spread out before their eyes on all sides scenes of beauty, changing with the change of seasons and changing every day; indeed the beauties of color and light and shade were changing at every stage of the day from the rosy dawn till the blue shades of evening came.

Yes, it was a delightful land and the people rejoiced in it. But a strange thing happened which caused the people to move away to a far-distant place. And this is the way it happened:

There was living in this village an old man, a wise man, a man who was held in great respect by the people, for he was a holy man, to whom the Unseen Powers granted knowledge not given to all the people. And these revelations came to the holy man in visions.

This holy man was now too old and feeble to till the soil and raise crops of food plants, or to go on the chase for game, or to gather any of the wild food plants. But because the young men held him in honor, they were glad to provide for him, and the women cooked for him of the best they had.

But he once had a vision which made him very sad, so that he could only cry and weep and could not speak of his vision for sadness of heart. And the people besought him to tell them his vision, for, they said, "if it is a vision of evil to come, we may as well know the worst; we ought to be prepared for it." For a long time the old man could not bring himself to tell them the evil foreboding which had come to him. But at last, when they continued strongly urging him to tell them what it was, he said: "Well, my children, I will tell you the vision, for it may be that I shall not live long. This vision has come to me from the Mysterious and Awful Powers, and it is full of evil portent for our people." But now he was again so overcome by sadness that he was unable to tell it.

Again, after some days, the people begged him to tell the vision, and they pressed him so urgently that finally he said: "This is what I saw in my vision, which has come to me repeatedly. I saw a great incursion of human beings of strange appearance. They are coming from the direction of the rising sun and are moving toward this land in multitudes so great that they cannot be counted. They move everywhere over the face of the land like the restless fluctuations of heated air which are sometimes seen incessantly wavering over the heated prairie on a summer day. They are moving on resistlessly toward us, and nothing can stop them, and they will take our land from us. They are a terrible people and of a monstrous appearance. The skin of this people is not of a wholesome color like the skin of our people who are born of our holy Mother Earth. Their skin is hideous and pale and ghastly, and the men have hairy faces like the face of a wolf. They are not kind like our people; they are savages, cruel and unfeeling. They have no reverence for our holy places, nor for our holy Mother Earth. And they kill and destroy all things and make the land desolate. They have no ear for the voices of the trees and the flowers, and no pity for the birds and the beasts of the field. And they deface and spoil the beauty of the land and befoul the water courses.

"And they have many dreadful customs. When a person dies, the body is not honorably laid upon a funeral scaffold on the prairie or in the branches of a tree in the forest, but they dig a hole in the ground and put the body down into the hole and then fill the hole up again, throwing the dirt down upon the body. And they have strange and powerful weapons, so that when they come our people will not be able to withstand them. It is this dreadful vision which has overcome me with sadness."

Then the people were amazed and angry. They tried to have him change his vision, but he could not. Again the same vision came to him. The leading men now counseled and gave order that the people should give him no more food for some days. They said, "Perhaps he will have a different vision." So he was left alone in his tent for four days. And on the fourth day, when they came to his tent, they found him dead. They had not intended to cause his death, but they hoped that if they let him become very hungry he would change his vision.

Now when they found him dead, they were shocked and astonished and very angry. They said, "Now the evil which he foretold will come, for he died without changing his vision." And they said, "We will not bury him honorably upon a scaffold according to the custom of the Dakotas, but we will bury him in a hole in the ground, as he said his 'wandering people' bury their dead." So they dug a hole, and into this they put the body of the old man, and they put the earth back again upon the body.

At evening some women were gazing out across the river in the twilight, and they saw a man come up out of the river and advance toward the village. When he came nearer, they saw it was the holy man who had died and whose body had been buried in a hole in the ground. When he died, he had changed from this life to the life of those who dwell in "The Land of Evening Mirage." From the place where they buried him, he had gone out under the ground, and he had come up out of the water of the river. Now when he came up out from the water, he was changed back again to life on earth. From this it was evident to all the people that he was indeed a very holy man, and that his vision was true and must come to pass. They gave him a good dwelling and provided for all his needs, and the women cooked for him the best food they had, and every one did homage to him and paid him reverence.

After a time he knew that the end of his life was approaching, and as he was about to die he called the leading men about him and said, "The vision which I had will truly come to pass in future time.

Now I am about to die. When I am dead, let me be buried in the ground again at the place where I was buried before. You will see that some good thing will come of it for our people at this place. And it shall be good for all people at this place forever." When he said something good would come, they thought he meant that the people should be saved from the cruel and savage, strange, pale-skinned people of his vision, but that was not what he meant.

When the holy man was dead, they would have preferred to give him honorable scaffold burial as was customary, but they did as he had directed and buried him in the ground where he had been buried before. But this time, they dug out a roomy place, and made walls and a roof with timbers, and in this place they put the body of the holy man after dressing him in the best of garments, decorated with porcupine quill embroidery, and wrapping him in a fine buffalo robe painted with beautiful designs. And they placed with him food and valuable presents of all kinds and his pipe and tobacco. Then they covered all with earth again and set the sod as it was before.

At evening they watched the place in the river where he had reappeared the other time after his burial. They thought he might return again out of the water of the river, but he did not come. And they listened above the little house they had made for him under the ground, but they heard not the slightest sound of breathing or any movement. Then they made a sacred fire by the grave from twigs of the cedar tree, for this tree is holy and sacred to the Good Powers, and the breath of its fire will bring persons of good intention into communion with those Unseen Powers. But the holy man did not appear by the sacred fire, and he was never seen again by any of the people.

Now the people became so burdened with sadness that they could not endure to remain at this place, and so they moved far away, where they found another good country. In this new place they stayed until all the people who were grown when they left the village of the holy man's grave had become old and had died. And none had ever been back there. Then, when all those who were but boys and girls when they left the former village had become old men and women, their tribe began to suffer harassment from an enemy people of another tribe. Their enemies were too strong for them, and so they had to think of moving to another place. And so it came into their minds to return to the place by the Muddy Water River, where they had lived at the time when those of their people who were now old had been merry, happy children.

So they came back. Before they had reached the place, the old men said, "Let us go on ahead and see the grave of the holy man." And when the old men came to the place where the holy man had been buried, they found that a spring of good water issued from the place where the holy man's grave had been. And that is why we call this spring "The Holy Man's Water Spring."

And it is said that now a bright star is often seen shining over this spring for a while and that it then goes down and disappears into the water of the spring. And it is said that sometimes when the moon is full and bright the holy man may be seen walking near the spring. When one approaches to speak to him, he disappears into the spring. Not all persons can see these things, but only those whose hearts are kind and gentle, and whose minds are in accord with Nature, and who have reverence for holy things and for the beauties and mysteries in Nature.

THE LEGEND OF STANDING ROCK

This story of Standing Rock is a legend of the Arikaras, who once had their villages along the Missouri River between the Grand River and the Cannon Ball River. Afterwards, being harassed by hostile incursions of the Dakotas, they abandoned this country to their enemies and moved farther up the Missouri River, joining themselves in alliance with the Mandans.

There was once a young girl in the Arikara tribe who was beautiful and amiable and not given to heedless, chattering, idle amusement. She was thoughtful and earnest, and was conversant with the ways of all the living creatures—the birds and the small mammals and the trees and shrubs and flowers of the woodlands and the prairies. She was in the habit of going to walk by herself to visit and commune with all these living creatures. She understood them better than most people did, and they all were her friends.

When she became of marriageable age she had many suitors, for she was beautiful and lovely in disposition. But to the young men who wooed her she answered, "I do not find it in my heart to marry anyone. I am at home with the bird people, the four-footed people of the woods and prairies, the people of the flower nations and the trees. I love to work in the cornfields in summer, and the sacred squash blossoms are my dear companions."

Finally, her grandmother reasoned with her and told her that it was her duty to marry and to rear children to maintain the strength of the tribe. Because of filial duty she finally said, when her grandmother continued to urge her to marry a certain young man of estimable worth who desired her for his wife, "Well, grandmother, I will obey you, but I tell you that good will not come of it. I am not as others are, and Mother Nature did not intend me for marriage."

So she was married and went to the house already prepared for her by her husband. But three days later she came back to her mother's house, appearing sad and downcast. She sat down without speaking. Finally her grandmother said, "What is it, my child? Is he not kind to you?" The girl answered, "Oh, he is not unkind. He treated me well." And with that she sped away into the forest. Her grandmother followed her after a little while, thinking that out among her beloved trees and plants she might open her heart and tell what was the trouble. And this she did, explaining all the trouble to her grandmother. And she concluded her talk with her grandmother with these words: "And so you see, grandmother, it is as I said when you urged me to marry. I was not intended for marriage. And now my heart is so sad. I should not have married. My spirit is not suited to the bounds of ordinary human living, and my husband is not to be blamed. He is honorable and kind. But I must go away and be with the children of nature." So her grandmother left her there where she was sitting by a clump of chokecherries, having her sewing kit with her and her little dog by her side.

She did not return home that night, and so the next morning young men were sent to search for her. At last she was found sitting upon a hill out on the prairie, and she was turned to stone from her feet to her waist. The young men hastened back to the village and reported to the officers who had sent them out.

Then the people were summoned by the herald, and they all went out to the place where the young woman was. Now they found she had become stone as far up as her breasts.

Then the priests opened the sacred bundle and took the sacred pipe, which they filled and lighted, and they presented it to her lips, so that thus she and they in turn smoking from the same pipe might be put in communion and accord with the spirit. But she refused the pipe and said, "Though I refuse the pipe, it is not from disloyalty or because of unwillingness to be at one with my people; but I am different by nature. And you shall know my good will towards my people and my love and remembrance of them always, for whoever places by this stone in summer time a wild flower, or in winter time a twig of a living tree, or any such token of living, wonderful Nature at any time, shall be glad in his heart, and shall have his desire to be in communion with the heart of Nature." And as she said these words she turned completely into stone, and her little dog, sitting at her feet and leaning close against her, was also turned into stone with her. And this stone is still to be seen, and is revered by the people. It is from this stone that the country around Fort Yates, North Dakota, is called Standing Rock.

THE HOLY HILL PAHOK

Each of the nations and tribes of Indians had certain places within its own domain which it regarded as sacred, and to which, accordingly, becoming reverence was paid. These places were sometimes water springs, sometimes peculiar hills, sometimes caves,

sometimes rocky precipices, sometimes dark, wooded
bluffs. Within the ancient domain of the Pawnee
nation, in Nebraska and northwest Kansas, there is a
group of five such sacred places. The chief one of
these five mystic places is called Pahok by the
Pawnees. From its nature it is unique, being distinctly different from any other hill in all the
Pawnee country. Pahok stands in a bend of the
Platte River, where the stream flows from the west,
sweeping abruptly toward the southeast. The head
of the hill juts out into the course of the river like
a promontory or headland, which is the literal meaning of the Pawnee word *pahok*. The north face of
the bluff, from the water's edge to the summit, is
heavily wooded. Among the trees are many cedars,
so that in winter, when the deciduous trees are bare,
the bluff is dark with the mass of evergreen cedar.
The cedar is a sacred tree, so its presence adds mystery to the place. The Pawnees sometimes also
speak of this hill as Nahurak Waruksti, which
means Sacred, or Mysterious, Animals. This allusion to the Mysterious Animals has reference to the
myth which pertains to this place.

All the other tribes throughout the Great Plains
region also know of the veneration in which this hill
is held by the Pawnees, so they, too, pay it great respect, and many individuals of the other tribes have
personally made pilgrimages to this holy place. The
people of the Dakota nation call it Paha Wakañ, the
Holy Hill.

The Pawnees speak of the animal world collectively as Nahurak. It was believed that the interrelations of all living beings—plants, animals and human beings—are essentially harmonious, and that all species take a wholesome interest in each other's welfare. It was believed also that, under certain conditions, ability was given to different orders of living creatures to communicate with men for man's good.

The before mentioned five sacred places of the Pawnee country were Nahurak lodges. Within these mystic secret places the animals, *nahurak*, held council. According to one version, the names of the five Nahurak lodges are Pahok, Nakiskat, Tsuraspako, Kitsawitsak, and Pahua. Pahok is a bluff on the south side of the Platte River, a few miles west of the city of Fremont, Nebraska; Nakiskat ("Black Trees") is an island in the Platte River near Central City, Nebraska, dark with cedar trees; Tsuraspako ("Girl Hill") is a hill on the south side of the Platte River opposite Grand Island, Nebraska. It is called Girl Hill because it was customary when a "buffalo surround" was made in its vicinity for the young girls to stay upon this hill during the surround. The hill is said to be in the form of an earth lodge, even to the extended vestibule. Kitsawitsak, which white people call Wakonda Springs, is not far from the Solomon River, near Beloit, Kansas. The name Kitsawitsak means "Water on the Bank." Pahua is said to be a spring near the

Republican River in Nebraska. Of these five places, Pahok was chief, and the Nahurak councils of the other lodges acknowledged the superior authority of the council at Pahok.

There are many stories of the wonderful powers resident in these sacred places. One of these tells of the restoration to life of a boy who had been killed. The story is that a certain man of the Skidi tribe of the Pawnee nation desired to gain the favor of Tirawa (Pawnee name of God). He thought that if he sacrificed something which he valued most highly, Tirawa might grant him some wonderful gift. There were so many things in the world which he did not understand, and which he wished very much to know. He hoped that Tirawa might grant him revelations, that he might know and understand many things which were hidden from the people. He strongly desired knowledge, and he thought that if he sacrificed his young son, who was dear to him, and the pride of his heart, Tirawa might take pity on him and grant him his desire. He felt very sad to think of killing his son, and he meditated a long time upon the matter. Finally he was convinced in his own mind that Tirawa would be pleased with his sacrifice, that then the good gifts he desired would be given to him, that many things now dark to his understanding would be made clear, and that he should have ability given him to do many things which were now beyond his power.

One day this man took his boy with him and

walked out from the village as though on some errand. They walked to the Platte River. After they had gone a long distance from the village, as they were walking by the riverside, no other persons being near, the man drew out his knife and stabbed the boy so that he was quickly dead. The man then dropped the body of the dead boy over the bank. After a time he returned to the village and went into his own lodge and sat down. He asked his wife, "Where is the boy?" She said, "Why, he went out with you." The man said, "I was out of the village, but the boy was not with me."

He went out and inquired of his neighbors, and then all through the village, but of course the boy could not be found. Then for some days a general search was made for the boy, but there was no trace of him. After this the family mourned for the lost boy. It was now time for the summer buffalo hunt, so in a few days the people set out for the buffalo grounds, and the father and mother of the boy were among them.

After the boy's body was dropped into the river, it was carried away downstream by the current, sometimes being rolled along in shallow water at the edge of sandbars, and again being turned over and over in the whirlpool of some deep hole in the channel, for the Platte River is a peculiar stream, having a swift current but a wide course with deep holes and many sandbars.

After a time the body floated down nearly to

Pahok. Two buzzards were sitting on the edge of a bluff, gazing over the water. So, sitting there, one of the buzzards stretched out his neck and looked up the river. He thought he saw something in the water, floating downstream. He stretched his neck again and looked, and turned to the other buzzard and said, "I see a body." Then they both looked towards the object in the water, stretching out their necks and gazing intently. They saw that the object was the body of the boy. The first one said, "What shall we do about this?" The second one said, "Let us carry the body down to Pahok, to the hill where the Nahurak Waruksti are." So they both flew down to the floating body and got under it and lifted it upon their backs and carried it to the top of the bluff called Pahok, over the secret cave of the Nahurak Waruksti, and there they placed it upon the ground. Then the two buzzards stood quietly gazing upon the body of the boy where they had laid it down upon the ground.

This cave far under the hill was the council lodge of the animals. There sat the councilors of all the kinds of animals and birds, great and small, which were native to that country. There were the buffalo, bear, elk, deer, antelope, otter, muskrat, wolf, fox, wildcat, badger, bean mouse and many other kinds of animals. And there were the swan, loon, goose, duck, wild turkey, prairie chicken, quail, heron, bittern, crane, plover, killdeer, meadow lark, blackbird, owl, hawk, swallow, crow, chickadee, woodpecker, grackle, purple martin and many other kinds of birds. There were also snakes, turtles, toads and frogs. These were the Nahurak people, the Nahurak Waruksti, the Sacred Animals. And the kingfisher was messenger and errand man for the Nahurak council.

Now it happened, when the buzzards brought the body of the young man and laid it down on the top of Pahok, that the kingfisher, who was flying over the river on business for the Nahurak, was flying by. He stopped and looked at the body. He already knew all that had happened, and he was moved with compassion for the boy. So he flew down at once to the water at the foot of Pahok and dived in at the entrance of the Nahurak lodge. He spoke to the assembly of the Nahurak and told them all that had happened. He said in conclusion: "And the poor boy is up there on the hill. I hope you will have pity on him and will do what you can for him. I wish you would bring him to life again." When the kingfisher, the messenger, had finished speaking, the Nahurak held serious council on the matter to decide what they should do. But after they had meditated long on the question, and each had spoken, they still could not decide. The kingfisher urged the matter, asking for a favorable decision, saying, "Come, do take pity on him and restore him to life." But they could not come to a decision. At last the chief of the council said: "No, messenger, we are unable to decide now. You must go to the other Nahurak lodges and find out what they have to say about it." The kingfisher said, "I go," and flew swiftly out from the lodge and up the river to Nakiskat, the Nahurak lodge near Lone Tree. There he brought the matter before the council, pleaded for the boy as he had done at Pahok, and told them that he was sent from Pahok to ask the council at Nakiskat for their decision. So the Nahurak here at Nakiskat talked over the matter, but at last they said to the kingfisher: "We are unable to decide. We leave it to the council at Pahok."

Then the kingfisher flew to the lodge at Tsuraspako, then to Kitsawitsak, and at last to Pahua, and at each place the Nahurak council considered the matter carefully and talked about it, but at each place the same answer was given. They all said, "It is too much for us. We cannot decide what should be done. It is for the council at Pahok to decide."

After the messenger had visited all these lodges and had laid the matter before all of them, receiving from each the same answer, he flew as swiftly as he could back to the lodge at Pahok and reported what the other lodges had said. They all recognized the council at Pahok as the head council and referred the matter to them for decision. But it had already been once considered by this council, and so the matter was now brought before the supreme council at Pahok. This was a council of four chiefs of the Pahok council, who sat as judges to give final consideration and decision. These judges now reconsidered the matter, and finally, when they had talked it over, they said to the kingfisher, "Now messenger, we will not decide this question, but will leave it to you. You shall make the decision."

The kingfisher very quickly gave his decision. He said, "It is my desire that this poor boy be restored to life. I hope you will all have pity on him and do what you can for him."

Then all the Nahurak arose and went out from the council lodge and went up to the top of Pahok where the body of the boy lay. They formed in order, stood around the boy and prayed to the Higher Powers. At last the boy drew breath; then after a time he breathed again; and then his breath began to be regular. Finally he opened his eyes, sat up, and looked around in a confused manner. When he saw all the animals standing around him he was puzzled and bewildered. He said to himself, "Why, my father killed me by the riverside, but here I am in the midst of this multitude of animals. What does it mean?"

Then the head chief of the Nahurak council spoke to him kindly and reassured him. He was asked to rise and go with the animals into the council lodge. When all had gone in and were seated, the four judges conferred together. The chief of the four stood up and said, "My people, we have restored this boy to life, but he is poor and forlorn and needy. Let us do something for him. Let us teach him all we know, and impart to him our mysterious powers." The Nahurak were all pleased at this proposal and manifested their approval.

Then the Nahurak showed hospitality and kind attention to the poor boy. He was shown a place to bathe and rest. When he had rested, food was brought to him. So he was entertained and treated kindly for the full season, and he was instructed by all the animals in turn; they taught him their secret arts of healing and imparted to him all their wonderful powers. So he remained with them at Pahok till autumn.

Autumn is a beautiful season at Pahok, and in all the region of the Platte, the Loup, the Republican, and the Soloman rivers in Nebraska and Kansas, which includes the group of the five Nahurak lodges. At that season in that country the sun casts a mellow golden light from the sky, while the land is emblazed with the brilliance of the sunflowers and goldenrod. And then the air is quiet and restful.

So one day at this season the Nahurak said to the boy: "It is now the time when the swallows, the blackbirds, the meadow larks, and other kinds of birds will be gathering into flocks to fly away to the southland for the winter. The beavers are cutting trees and saplings to store the branches under water for their winter food supply of bark; they are also gathering into their houses certain kinds of roots for food. The muskrats are repairing their houses and

are storing in them the tubers of the water lilies and
of the arrowleaf and of other kinds of plants for
their winter supply. In the edge of the timber,
where the ground beans grow, the bean mice are
making their storehouses and filling them with
ground beans and artichokes. And your people have
returned from the buffalo hunt with a good supply
of dried meat and hides. They are now busy at
home gathering and storing their crops of corn, of
beans, and of squashes and pumpkins. We have this
past summer instructed you in our arts of healing
and other learning, and have imparted to you our
mysterious powers, and have taught you about our
ways of living. You are now competent to use for
the good of your people the remedies and to perform the mysteries which were given to us by
Tirawa, and which we have now given to you. So
you may now return to the village of your people.
Go to the chiefs of the village and tell them what
the Nahurak have done for you, and say to them
that the people are to bring together gifts of dried
buffalo meat and dried corn and dried chokecherries
and other kinds of food; of robes and leggings and
moccasins embroidered with porcupine quills; and
of tobacco for incense. All these things the people
are to send by you as gifts to the Nahurak at Pahok
in recognition of the favor which the Nahurak
showed to you."

So the boy parted from his animal friends at
Pahok, and promised to return and visit them and to

bring them presents to show his thankfulness and the thankfulness of his people for what the animals had done for him. He traveled on up the Platte River and reached the village of his people in the night. He went to his father's house. He found his father and mother asleep, and the fire had burned low. There was only a little light from the coals. He went to his mother's bed and touched her shoulder and spoke to her to waken her. He said, "It is I. I have come back." When his mother saw him and heard his voice she was surprised, but she was glad-hearted to see her boy again. So she wakened the boy's father and told him the boy had come back. When the father saw the boy, he thought it must be a ghost, and he was afraid. But the boy did not mention anything that had happened nor say where he had been. He said only, "I have come back again."

The next day some of the people saw him, and they were surprised. They told their neighbors, and soon it was rumored all over the village that the boy had returned. They came where he was and stood around and looked at him and asked him questions, but he told them nothing. But he went to the chiefs of the village and made his report to them. Afterwards he gave account to the people, saying, "I have been away all summer with friends, with people who have been very good to me. Now I should like to take them a present of dried meat and other good things, so that we can have a feast. I beg you to help me, my friends." So they brought together a quantity of the articles required, and they chose some young men to go with him to help carry the gifts to the people who had befriended him.

So the boy and his companions went on the way towards the Nahurak lodge at Pahok. When they came near to the place, the boy dismissed the young men who had accompanied him, and they went back to the village. Now the boy went on alone and met the kingfisher and sent word by this messenger of the Nahurak that he had come to visit them and had brought presents from his people. So the boy was invited into the lodge, and all the Nahurak made sounds of gladness at seeing him again. The boy brought in the presents which had been sent by his people, and the Nahurak had a feast. After the feast they held a doctors' ceremony. They reviewed all the things that the Nahurak had taught him during the summer that he had spent with them. Then the boy was made a doctor, and he was now able to do many wonderful things.

After this the time came for the young man to return again to the village of his people. The animals were thankful and gave praise to Tirawa for the gifts which the young man had brought to them. And the young man was thankful to the animals, and he praised Tirawa for what the animals had done for him. Then he returned to the village of his people. He never told the people what his father had done to him.

The young man lived a long and useful life among his people and attained much honor. He did many wonderful things for them and healed them of their diseases and injuries. In time he gathered about him a group of other young men who, like himself, were of serious and thoughtful mind, and who had desire toward the welfare of the people. These young men became his disciples, and to them he taught the mysteries which had been imparted to him by the animals of the lodge at Pahok. These wise men in turn taught other worthy inquirers, and these again taught others; and so these mysteries and this learning and the healing arts have come down from that long ago time to the present among the Pawnee people.

LOVE OF THE HOMELAND

In the rituals of the various tribes may be found numerous expressions of the love and reverence which the people had for Holy Mother Earth and for their own homeland in particular. In their thought of their homeland they did not regard it as a possession which they owned, but they regarded themselves as possessed by their homeland, their country, to which they owed love and service and reverence.

Part II of the Twenty-second Annual Report of the Bureau of American Ethnology includes an ancient ritual of the Pawnee nation, recorded in full by Miss Alice Fletcher. The old Pawnee country extended from the Solomon River, in what is now the state of Kansas, northward across the drainage systems of the Republican, the Platte and the Loup and to the Niobrara River, in the northern part of what is now the state of Nebraska. In this ancient ritual occurs this song which very plainly reflects the appearance of the country of the Pawnee nation in that part of the Great Plains which I have just defined. In the song we can sense the lively affection which the Pawnees had for their dear Motherland, the land in which their people had lived for many centuries, where they and uncounted generations of their ancestors had labored in growing their agricultural crops and in the harvest of the wild crops, the native fruits of the land.

SONG TO THE TREES AND STREAMS

I

Dark against the sky yonder distant line
Lies before us. Trees we see, long the line of trees,
Bending, swaying in the breeze.

II

Bright with flashing light yonder distant line
Runs before us, swiftly runs, swift the river runs,
Winding, flowing o'er the land.

III

Hark! O hark! A sound, yonder distant sound,
Comes to greet us, singing comes: soft the river's song,
Rippling gently 'neath the trees.

In this song one can hear the constant murmur of the summer south wind as it blows in that country for days, and can see the broad stretch of the great level land, gently undulating in places, with its eastward-flowing streams bordered by zones of trees, the timbered zones along the stream courses being the only forest land in that country.

THE SPIRIT OF LIFE

Among Indians generally, as I have known them in a number of different tribes or nations, there is a common feeling of reverence for life in all its forms, whether that life be manifest in human form, in the various species of animals, or in plants. They think of all living creatures—men, animals and plants—as partners in the wonderful and mysterious quality of life. They teach their children to have respect for all living things, however lowly.

In the Sacred Legend of the Arikara nation there are precepts of this kind. One such makes reference to the ants, to their habitations and habits of life, saying: "Thus we are taught that the ants and all living creatures, even though small and humble and seemingly insignificant, yet have their own proper place in the world, and they are endowed with the mysterious attribute, life, even as we are. So they are our partners in this living world, they are our relatives, and we should treat them with respect."

Indians also gave reverence to the elements of the universe, such as the sunshine, which is the life-giving energy; to the winds, the air, which is the breath of life; and to living water, the water of life in lakes and streams. Devout persons would often voice in prayers of gratitude and appreciation their pious contemplations of the wonders of nature.

The body of teaching which I have here called the Sacred Legend of the Arikaras is the unwritten Holy Bible of that people, handed down through uncounted generations from the pious and wise men of their nation in the ancient time. Other tribes also have their own Sacred Legends or Bibles, imprinted in the hearts and bound in the memory of the priests and teachers of their cults.

CHILDREN OF MOTHER EARTH

People of European race resident in America (Americans, we call ourselves) have sentimental regard toward the plants and animals native to Europe, some of which, domesticated by our ancestors, we have brought with us to America. But most of our people have not developed such sentiments toward the plants and animals native to America. Literary allusions, songs and stories refer to trees, flowers, birds and other forms of life pertaining to our old home lands in Europe, but not to those of America. People of our race have been inhabitants of America now for three centuries, and still we have not made ourselves at home here; we have not formed sentimental attachment to the land and to its native forms of life.

It is a pity for a people not to be so attached to the country in which they live that their sentiments shall be first of all for the forms of life that are native to their own country; the disharmony lessens happiness and is hurtful in many ways.

Lacking friendly feeling for the plants and animals native to America, we have destroyed these things in a ruthless manner; and this can hardly be prevented by law unless we can awaken sentiment for the native forms of life in America such as that which our ancestors had for forms of life native in Europe.

Indians, the native Americans, have friendly sentiments, and even feelings of reverence, for the forms of life native to America.

Indians generally were shrewd and discerning observers of the life and habits of plants and animals. The careful study of plants and animals was a considerable part of the courses of study in their system of education, which included much more than is supposed by persons who have not made themselves acquainted with Indian life. They were well informed in plant and animal ecology, and in knowledge of range of species. They took cognizance of the habits of animals in the animals' dwelling places. An old Indian once told me how a muskrat lays up stores of food in his house. He compared the appearance of a muskrat's stores to that of a grocer's goods on the shelves of his store. Many old Indians have told me what kinds of food are stored by different species of animals. Indians often speak of those species of animals which lay up food stores as being civilized animal nations, and of those which do not make such provision as being uncivilized.

Indians attribute great wisdom to certain species of animals. This disposition results from discerning observation of the animals' works and ways. The beaver, notably, is reputed to be very wise and industrious. Indians often sought to gain the favor and learn the wisdom of various animal species by endeavoring to place themselves in sympathetic and harmonious relationship with the guardian genius of each species.

With regard to the native animals and plants, the attitude of mind of white people is fundamentally different from that of Indians. The attitude of white people generally seems to be that the extinction of a species of plant or animal is a matter of indifference except for the consideration of its desirability for use or for pleasure. The thought of preserving the balance of nature does not sway the minds of most white people. But this is the consideration which, to the Indian mind, is of prime importance.

Most white men are unable to appreciate or to comprehend the grief and pain experienced by Indians when they see the native forms of life in

America ruthlessly and wantonly destroyed. It was not primarily the realization of economic loss, the loss of a valuable source of food, which caused distress to Indians when, for instance, they witnessed the destruction of wild rice fields and lotus beds, but it was the sense of a fearful void in nature ensuing upon the extinction of a given species where it had formerly flourished. They were pained to contemplate the dislocation of nature's nice balance, the destruction of world symmetry.

I have been told many times, by different persons of various tribes, of the teaching concerning the sanctity of life which they received in their childhood. They tell me that they were taught by their parents and elders that plants and animals must not be destroyed needlessly, that wanton destruction is wicked. A precept which they frequently heard was:

"Do not needlessly destroy the flowers on the prairie or in the woods. If the flowers are plucked, there will be no flower babies (seeds); and if there be no flower babies, then in time there will be no people of the flower nations. And if the flower nations die out of the world, then the earth will be sad. All the flower nations and all the different nations of living things have their own proper places in the world, and the world would be incomplete and imperfect without them."

I once asked an old Omaha what was the feeling of Indians when they saw white men wantonly slaughtering the buffalo. He dropped his head and was silent for a little while, seeming to be overcome by a feeling of sadness. When he spoke again it was in a low, sad tone, seeming filled with shame that such a thing could be done by human beings. He said:

"It seemed to us a most wicked, awful thing."

Again I was talking with an old man of the Omaha nation. He, recalling the old days and comparing them with the present time, said:

"When I was a youth, the country was very beautiful. Along the rivers were belts of timberland, where grew cottonwood, maple, elm, ash, hickory and walnut trees, and many other kinds. Also there were various kinds of vines and shrubs. And under these grew many good herbs and beautiful flowering plants. In both the woodland and the prairie I could see the trails of many kinds of animals and could hear the cheerful songs of many kinds of birds. When I walked abroad I could see many forms of life, beautiful living creatures which Wakanda had placed here; and these were, after their manner, walking, flying, leaping, running, playing all about. But now the face of all the land is changed and sad. The living creatures are gone. I see the land desolate, and I suffer an unspeakable sadness. Sometimes I wake in the night and I feel as though I should suffocate from the pressure of this awful feeling of loneliness."

NATURE AND HEALTH

The philosophy of health and wholesomeness of the native Americans, the Indians, was to live in accordance with nature and by coming as much as possible into direct physical contact with the elements in nature, such as the sunshine, the rain and snow, the air and earth. They felt the need and desire to be in frequent and immediate contact with Mother Earth, to receive upon their persons the strong rays of the sun and the restorative efficacy of the winds from the clean sky, and to bathe daily in living streams.

The priest of a certain ritual of the Pawnee nation visited Washington. He admired the Washington monument as he viewed it from the Capitol. When he went over to visit the monument, he measured the dimensions of its base by pacing; then he stood and gazed towards its summit, noting its height. Then he went inside; but when he was asked whether he would walk up the stairway or go on the lift, he said: "I will not go up. White men like to pile up stones, and they may go to the top of them; I will not. I have ascended the mountains made by Tirawa." *Tirawa* is the Pawnee name of God.

Some years ago Mr. Louis J. Hill took a party of people of the Blackfoot tribe to New York City as his guests. They were interested in the sight of the great engineering feats as manifested in the great structures of the city. But they were unwilling to be cooped up in the rooms of the hotel; so they made arrangements to be allowed to set up their tents upon the hotel roof so that they might at least have the natural sunlight and the outdoor air.

In an ancient Pawnee ritual there is a hymn which begins with the words, "Now behold; hither comes the ray of our father Sun; it cometh over all the land, passeth in the lodge, us to touch, and give us strength." And in another stanza of this hymn, referring to the passing of the sun, it continues, "Now behold where alights the ray of our father Sun; around the lodge the ray has passed and left its blessing there, touching us, each one of us."

So it was ever the aim to live in accord with nature, to commune often with nature. A word of admonition from the wisdom lore of the Menomini tribe says, "Look often at the moon and the stars." And the Winnebagos have a wise saying: "Holy Mother Earth, the trees and all nature are witnesses of your thoughts and deeds." Another admonition of Winnebago wisdom is: "Reverence the Unseen Forces that are always near you and are always trying to lead you right."

THE BREAKING UP OF THE ICE

It is said that in the long ago there was a mysterious being within the stream of the Missouri River. It was seldom seen by human beings, and was most dreadful to see. It is said that sometimes it was seen within the water in the middle of the stream, causing a redness shining like the redness of fire as it passed up the stream against the current with a terrific roaring sound.

And they say that if this dreadful being was seen by anyone in the daytime, he who thus saw it became crazy soon after and continued restless and writhing as though in pain until he was relieved by death. And it is said that one time not a very great many years ago this frightful being was seen by a man, and he told how it appeared. He said that it was of strange form and covered all over with hair like a buffalo, but red in color; that it had only one eye in the middle of its forehead, and above that a single horn. Its backbone stood out notched and jagged like an enormous saw. As soon as the man beheld the awful sight, everything became dark to him, he said. He was just able to reach home, but he lost his reason, and soon afterward he died.

It is said that this mysterious water monster still lives in the Missouri River, and that in springtime, as it moves upstream against the current, it breaks up the ice of the river. This water monster was held in awe and dread by the Dakota people.

A MANDAN MONUMENT

It is a common instinct among all nations of the human race to preserve relics and build memorials of notable persons and events. Such monuments vary with the different means and materials at hand. Sometimes mounds of earth, sometimes boulders, sometimes cairns of stones, sometimes hewn stones, and various other devices have been used according to circumstances.

There exists a monument to the memory of a Mandan hero which has never before been described. The following account is from information given by several persons of the Mandan, Hidatsa and Arikara tribes. The location of the monument is near the site of Fishhook Village, on the north side of the Missouri River, some twelve or fifteen miles east of Elbowoods, North Dakota.

During the middle part of the nineteenth century the three tribes, Arikara, Hidatsa and Mandan, lived together in alliance against their common enemies. Their chief enemies were the Dakotas. So these three tribes built their three villages adjoining, making one compound village of three wards. The village lay upon a well-drained terrace of the Missouri River, while the farms were laid out in the fertile alluvial bottom along the river both above and below the village. To the north of the village site lies a range of hills.

The enemy many times made raids upon the village. They would approach under cover of the hills to the north and then steal close upon the village through the course of a ravine which skirted the northeast and north sides of the village.

About the year 1853 such an attack was made by a war party of Dakotas. Of the defenders of the village, two young Mandans, brothers, named Lefthand and Redleaf, had been dismounted, and their retreat had been cut off by the enemy. A brother of these two, Whitecrow by name, saw the danger of Lefthand and Redleaf and rode out to their assistance. Lefthand was killed and Redleaf was defending the body from a Dakota who was trying to take the scalp. Redleaf shot at the Dakota and missed him, the bullet going over the enemy's head and striking into the ground beyond him, the enemy being crouched low at the time of the shot. Whitecrow rode in a circuit beyond these combatants and held off the attacking party of the enemy. He killed the Dakota who was engaged in combat with his brother Redleaf. Then Whitecrow lifted Redleaf upon the horse with himself and carried him safely back to the village.

After the enemy had been driven away, the Mandans went out and marked the course in which Whitecrow had ridden to his brother's rescue, the spot where Lefthand had been killed, the spot where Redleaf had made his stand, the spot where the Dakota was killed, and the spot where Redleaf's bullet, fired at the Dakota, had struck the ground. The method used for marking these places was by removal of the sod, leaving holes in the ground. To mark the course of Whitecrow's horse, the sod was removed in sections shaped like horse tracks, from the point of advance from the village, round the place of combat, and returning to the village. The horse-track marks were made about two feet in diameter. All these marks commemorating the entire action are still plainly evident, being renewed whenever they tend to become obliterated by weathering and by advancing vegetation.

LODGE AND TIPI

A BOY'S EDUCATION

In the Dakota nation in old times in all respectable families the parents took care and gave thought and study to the matter of the home training and education of their children. Parents loved their children and did not carelessly leave them to stray about the neighborhood without counsel and guidance and without oversight of their companionship and occupations. Loving parents, having proper family pride, looked after their children and kept them at home or allowed them to go out in suitable company when they knew where they were going and what they were doing. They impressed upon their children's characters the principle of family pride, and children in respectable families were inclined to heed the counsel of their parents and to give attention to their teaching.

Such parents dressed their children as well as their circumstances allowed, and provided them with elegant clothing for public occasions, so that the children would not feel themselves slighted or lacking in dignity. Thus the children, seeing that a respectable standard was set for them, would be disposed to hold themselves worthy.

A boy's best suit—tunic, breechcloth, leggings and moccasins—would be ornately embroidered with porcupine quills. Sometimes his best pair of moccasins would be decorated with porcupine quill embroidery even on the soles. When a boy became old enough, he would be given a first-class saddle horse. He was also given a saddle blanket decorated with quillwork. He was taught how to take care of his horse and outfit, and to have proper pride in keeping them in good condition. As a boy grew in stature and improved in knowledge and skill, more tasks and duties were laid upon him, so that he had occasion to feel that he was coming to be an individual of some worth and responsibility in the community. He was gradually brought to feel that he had a personal name and station to maintain. One of the earliest duties assigned to boys was the care of the family band of horses while they grazed upon the prairie.

A good and comfortable place in the lodge was assigned to each child for his own, and there he could keep his own things and feel that he had a place of some consideration. Thus was inculcated a feeling of personal dignity, a sense of obligation to maintain personal worth. The place assigned to a child in the lodge was his sleeping place at night and the place where he could sit whenever he was in the lodge in the daytime. A canopy decorated with painting was hung overhead at this place, and his bed and personal belongings were kept in order. The personal belongings of a boy included a knife and decorated knife scabbard, an awl in a decorated awl case, a headdress, a hairbrush made of the needles of the needle grass, strips of otter skin to wrap his hair braids, and narrow strips of deer skin decorated with porcupine quills to tie the otter skin wrappings of his hair. He also was provided with a case of paints of various colors for decorating his person on occasions, and a wooden bowl and a buffalo-horn spoon for taking food. In such manner loving parents, caring for the proper rearing of their children, provided for them everything of the best that they could afford. So they did for their girls, as well as for their boys.

But it was not only in the provision of good clothing and food and personal comforts and ornaments that parents showed care and affection for their children. They also took care of their moral, intellectual, and social training. They would never use a whip on a child. That would be treating it like a slave or an irrational creature. They were careful not to subjugate or break the spirit of a child, making it slavelike and cringing. They would not scold or roughly reprove a child, but would admonish it gently and reasonably, careful not to hurt its feelings or wound its spirit. They thus taught their children to exercise their own powers of moral choice and responsibility.

Children were instructed at home in all the things that were needful for them in their station in life. They were taught and trained to skill in the crafts necessary for them to practice in adult life. They were taught the geography of their own country and of the countries of the neighboring tribes and nations. They were taught the elements of the botany and zoölogy of their region, the history and political organization of their own people, the linguistic principles and correct usages of their own language, and the codes of ethics and of etiquette of their people. They were taught and trained to have self-control and reserve in action and in speech, and to have proper respect for age and wisdom.

If a child lacked such careful home training, people would say that it was as if it had no parents, or that its parents did not care for it, and that it grew up like the wild animals. Such remarks would be a shame both to the parents and to the child.

Children of respectable and well-to-do parents would be made members of certain social organizations, and on occasions of public gatherings they were expected to take part and to make many gifts and to do their share in giving public entertainments and feasts. Thus they attained social recognition. On such occasions, when a horse was given, or some other valuable gift was made in the name of the child, of course it was so announced publicly by the herald. Besides the announcement made by the herald, recognition would be made by the recipient of the gift, who was usually some old person or poor, unfortunate person, who would step into the dancing-circle and there dance and sing the praise of the child as a generous and praiseworthy person. In all such ways self-respect and the sense of personal responsibility were cultivated and fostered in the children of good families.

THE CEREMONY OF HUNKA

The Dakota nation formerly had a custom by which marks of recognition and distinction were publicly conferred upon persons whose character and acts of public benefaction were esteemed worthy of honor. This custom was the institution of Hunka. The term *hunka* primarily means parent or ancestor. In the primary sense of the term, an elder brother might be termed *hunka* by his younger brothers and sisters, by reason of his favors and benefactions to them. The sun might be called *hunka,* from the beneficent effects of his radiance.

Any person who had become elevated in the esteem of the people in such degree as to be considered a public benefactor or parent to the community might be given this title. Thus the term was used as a title of respect, and those on whom it was conferred constituted socially an aristocracy within a community which, in political organization, was essentially democratic, for the Dakota form of government was quite democratic. In the Dakota nation, any social distinction was based upon personal character and worth; and positions of military and political leadership depended upon personal qualities of ability, force and tact.

All persons who themselves had been at some time made Hunka formed a sort of society or class. Recognition of any person as Hunka was made the occasion of public ceremony. Some family of good standing, and being of this rank, having a daughter come to marriageable age, might announce that they would hold the Hunka ceremony for her at a certain time. Such a ceremony then would be a sort of coming-out party for her.

A ceremonial tent was pitched within the camp circle. Its cover was opened at the front. Then an inclosure was erected as a screen before this open tent, to exclude the public gaze from what went on within. The walls of this enclosure extended forward for a distance of some yards at each side of the entrance to the ceremonial tent.

A good old man of high esteem in the community would be asked to officiate in the ceremony. He would be seated in the place of honor in the tent. A fire was laid in the fireplace; a bunch of wild sage (*Artemisia gnaphalodes*) was laid at the altar place; on the wild sage rested a buffalo skull; and at one side of this was an ear of corn. Before the buffalo skull was placed a pipe, filled with a preparation for smoking—a mixture of tobacco and the dried inner bark of the red dogwood (*Cornus stolonifera*), which erroneously often has been referred to as "red willow." A small horn spoon and a small wooden bowl containing a few bits of meat were placed within convenient reach of the old man where he sat in the place of honor.

Reputable and honorable persons were invited to assist by their presence. They were seated at the sides within the tent. The chorus of singers and drummers was seated in front of the tent, within the screened inclosure. Gifts were heaped up within this inclosure, and horses which were to be given away were tied just outside in front. Crowds of people thronged outside to see what they could, and also to be on hand for the receipt of any gifts which might come their way, if they were so fortunate, in the distribution of gifts after the ceremony.

The girl for whom the ceremony was made would be brought to the ceremonial tent from her domicile, carried on the shoulders of a man. The man who went to fetch the girl stooped before her, and she placed her arms about his neck. Another man assisted by lifting her feet from the ground and carrying them. So she was carried in and seated opposite the old man who officiated in the ceremony. He would then remove the girl's shawl from her shoulders and put upon her a fine new dress over the one which she was wearing. Then her hair was combed and a yellow down feather was tied in her hair on the top of her head. A new shawl was then draped over her shoulders.

The yellow down feather was an emblem, and its color was symbolic. Yellow suggests the radiance of the sun, the source of light and warmth and energy in the world, and symbolizes the aspiration for spiritual enlightenment and power, and the hope and joy and gladness of life.

After the girl's hair was combed and she was newly dressed, the old man gave her a lecture in which he exhorted her to the practice of the virtues of chastity, hospitality, industry, honesty, generosity and gentleness, to kindness to the old, the sick, the poor, and the needy, to compassion for distress, and to tenderness toward children. During the exhortation, she was ceremonially fed with the meat from the small wooden bowl, with the ceremonial horn spoon. The ceremony was concluded by the smoke offerings made by the old man with the pipe which was before the buffalo skull. After the close of the ceremony, the gifts were distributed to the people. The names of those to whom the gifts were made would be called out by the herald, and they would come forward and receive the gifts.

THE SACRED NUMBER FOUR

It appears that Great Spirit has caused everything in the world to be in fours; for this reason it is well that mankind's activities of all kinds should be governed by the number four in order to be in agreement and harmony with the evident plan of the world.

We see that there are four directions—east, south, west, and north; four divisions of time—the day, the night, the moon, and the year; four seasons —spring, summer, autumn, and winter; four parts to everything that grows from the ground—root, stem, leaf, and fruit; four kinds of creatures which breathe—those that crawl, those that fly, those that walk on four legs, and those that walk on two legs; four things above the earth—the sun, the moon, the sky, and the stars; four kinds of gods—the great gods, the associates of the great, the gods below them, and the spirits or genii of all the different species of plants and animals; four periods of human life—infancy, youth, adulthood, and old age; mankind has four fingers on each hand, four toes on each foot, and the thumbs and great toes taken together make four; a person presents four aspects to view—the front, the back, the left side, and the right side; a river has four parts—the surface, the bottom, the right bank, and the left bank; a flower has four parts—the calyx, the corolla, the stamens, and the pistils.

And so we could go on indefinitely with such enumeration of examples of the appearances of the number four throughout all nature. Everywhere we look, we see such appearances. So we think that all these tokens of the works of Great Spirit should cause mankind to order all ceremonies and activities by this sacred number for the sake of harmony.

THE SACRED SYMBOL OF THE CIRCLE

To the people of the Dakota nation, and probably also to the people of many other tribes, the circle is a sacred symbol, because Great Spirit caused everything in nature to be round except stone. And stone is the implement of destruction. The sun, the earth, and the moon are round like a shield, and the sky is round like a bowl inverted over the earth. All things growing out of the earth are round, as the trunk of a tree or the stem of grass or the stem of an herb. The human body also is round, and the bodies of all creatures which breathe are round like the human body. The members of the body, as the arm and the leg, are round. The edge of the world is a circle; hence the circle is a symbol of the world and of the winds which travel to us from all points on the edge of the world. The sun and the moon, which mark the day and the night, travel in circles above the sky; therefore the circle is a symbol of these divisions of time, and of the year, and so of all time.

Raindrops are round, and so are the drops of dew hanging as strings of beads upon the grass blades. Pellets of hail and of sleet are round. Every snowflake has a center from which lines radiate as from the center of a circle. The rainbow, which beautifies the sky after showers, is round.

Because Great Spirit has caused almost all things to be round, the circle is for us a sacred symbol; it reminds us of the works of Great Spirit in all the world. And for this reason people of the Dakota nation make their tipis round; and in laying a camp tipis are set in a circular line. In all ceremonies, the people sit in a circle, and the action in ceremonies is in a circle and from right to left as the sun moves in its daily path.

We observe those wonderful little creatures, the ants. There are many species of ants. Some make underground dwellings by excavating the earth and making tunnels and passages; others build up mounds upon the surface of the earth. Those kinds which dwell below the surface of the earth, we see carry out the soil they excavate and deposit it in a circle about the openings of their underground dwellings; and those which build mounds make these mounds circular at their bases.

The circle is a symbol of the tipi, and that suggests home and shelter and comfort. In decorative figures the undivided circle is a symbol of the world and of time. If the circle is filled with red, it is a symbol of the sun; if filled with blue, it is a symbol of the sky. If the circle be divided into four parts, it is a symbol of the four winds.

In formal or ceremonial smoking, the pipe should always be passed about the circle from right to left. The one who lights the pipe should offer the mouthpiece of the pipe toward the four directions in the circle of the earth before smoking and passing the pipe to his left-hand neighbor.

THE EARTH LODGE

As an example of the modifying power of geographic influence exercised upon the arts, we may consider the style of architecture or domiciliary structure prevailing in the Plains region. In each geographic province, which also constitutes a culture area, the style of housing is different according to natural resources and climatic conditions. In the Plains area, the permanent dwelling was the earth-covered structure, while the temporary dwelling was the skin tent.

The earth-covered house seems to be an evolution from the thatched house of the southern Plains, exemplified in the dwellings of the Wichitas. Farther north the exigencies of the climate suggested the addition of an earth covering.

All the nations and tribes of the Missouri, of whatever racial stock, employed the same style of dwelling. In order to effect the construction of an earth-covered house, a circle of the desired diameter

was stripped off from the surface soil.   Four tall,
strong forked posts were set in the center, about eight
or ten or twelve feet apart, in a quadrangle.   Beams
were laid on these forks. Outside of the center posts,
a circle of shorter posts was set, and beams were
laid in their forks. Rafters were laid from the lower
to the upper beams.   A wall of timbers was leaned
up against the circle of lower beams, the base of the
leaning timbers resting upon the ground.   An opening was left at the east, and here was made a vestibule from seven to fourteen feet long.

Timbers were laid upon the rafters, willow poles
were laid upon the timbers, and a thatch of dry grass
upon these poles.   A covering of earth was now
built up about the walls and over the roof to a total
thickness of about two feet, making, when complete,
a dome-shaped structure.

All structural timbers and poles were fastened by
tying with ropes of rawhide or of basswood or elm
fiber.

An opening of several feet in diameter was left
at the top of the dome for a skylight, ventilator, and
smoke escape.   The fireplace was at the center of
the earth floor; the sleeping compartments were
ranged about, next to the wall.   The altar was at
the west side, opposite the doorway.

The diameter of the house varied, according to
the needs of the family which occupied it, from
thirty to fifty or sixty feet; the height, from fifteen
to twenty feet.   This was a family domicile and not

a community or tenement house. Such family dwellings were clustered in villages. The evidences of many such village sites may be seen throughout all the region of the Missouri River drainage basin. The fields of agricultural crops were cultivated in alluvial valleys, usually near the villages, although sometimes, when suitable land was not near, the fields might be at some distance.

The earth-covered house probably originated with the tribes of Caddoan stock—that is, the Pawnees and Arikaras—and was adopted by the tribes of other stocks upon their migration into the Missouri River region.

The Pawnees had very elaborate ceremonies and traditions connected with the earth lodge. The earlier star cult is recognized in the signification attached to the four central posts. Each stood for a star—the Morning Star, and the Evening Star, symbols of the male and female cosmic forces, and the North and South Stars.

In the rituals of the Pawnees the earth lodge is made typical of man's abode on the earth: the floor is the plain; the wall, the horizon; the dome, the arching sky; the central opening, the zenith—the dwelling place of Tirawa, the invisible power which gives life to all creatures.

In the poetic thought of the Pawnees, the earth was regarded as Mother and was so called, because from the earth's bounty mankind is fed. To their imagination, the form of the earth lodge suggests

the figure of speech by which these human dwellings
were likened to a woman's breasts and symbolized
the breasts of Mother Earth; for here man is nour-
ished and nurtured, he is fed and sheltered and
blessed with the tendernesses of life.   Here he
knows love and warmth and gentleness.

Herewith is given a metrical translation of a
hymn extracted from the ritual of a ceremonial of
great age in the Pawnee nation.   There were similar
ceremonials among other tribes and nations of the
Plains area.   The full ritual from which this is
taken is published in the Twenty-second Annual Report of the Bureau of American Ethnology, Part II.
The allusions in the hymn to the structure of the
earth lodge will be readily understood.

HYMN TO THE SUN

I

Now behold: hither comes the ray of our father Sun;
   it cometh over all the land, passeth in the lodge,
   us to touch, and give us strength.

II

Now behold: where alights the ray of our father Sun;
   it touches lightly on the rim, the place above the fire,
   whence the smoke ascends on high.

III

Now behold: softly creeps the ray of our father Sun;
   now o'er the rim it creeps to us, climbs down within
   the lodge; climbing down, it comes to us.

IV

Now behold: nearer comes the ray of our father Sun;
it reaches now the floor and moves within the open
space, walking there, the lodge about.

V

Now behold where alights the ray of our father Sun;
around the lodge the ray has passed and left its
blessing there, touching us, each one of us.

VI

Now behold: softly climbs the ray of our father Sun;
it upward climbs, and o'er the rim it passes from the
place whence the smoke ascends on high.

VII

Now behold on the hills the ray of our father Sun:
it lingers there as loath to go, while all the plain
is dark. Now has gone the ray from us.

VIII

Now behold: lost to us the ray of our father Sun;
beyond our sight the ray has gone, returning to
the place whence it came to bring us strength.

THE TIPI

The temporary dwelling used for traveling was
a conical tent made from buffalo skins erected on a
frame of poles. It commonly had about twenty
poles averaging twenty-five feet long. The poles
were set in a circle about fifteen feet in diam-

eter, held together above by a hide rope wound
round the whole set of poles about four feet from
the upper ends. Three poles were first tied together; then the others were laid in the forks of
these; then the rope was passed round all of them
and tied. For the cover, from fifteen to eighteen
buffalo hides were cut and fitted so that, when
sewn together with sinew thread, they formed a
single large sheet nearly semicircular in shape. This
was lifted into place by a special pole at the back of
the structure. Then the ends were brought around
to the front and fastened by means of eight or ten
small wooden pins at intervals from the door to the
crossing of the poles. The bottom was kept in place
by pegs about two feet apart around the circle. The
door was usually a piece of skin stretched over an
elliptical frame.

At the top an opening was left for ventilation and
for outlet for the smoke of the fire. The draft was
regulated by two flaps or wings, each supported on
a movable pole slanted alongside the tipi with its
base on the ground and its top fastened to the apex
of the smoke flap. This held the draft open to the
side away from the wind and was moved according
to changes of the wind so as always to be open to
the lee side.

The beds were at the sides and the back of the
tipi. Decorated curtains above the beds kept off any
drops of rain which might come through the smoke
hole in rainy weather. The ground was the floor,

the part near the beds being sometimes cut off from the open space by a hedge of interwoven twigs.

In warm weather the bottom of the tipi was raised to allow the breeze to pass through. In cold weather the bottom was banked with grass to keep out the wind.

The camp was arranged in a circle. Each band of the tribe had its own proper segment of the circle, which was relatively the same through immemorial generations, and each family in each band had its proper place in the segment, so that one coming into camp after nightfall, although he might not have been in the camp before, could thus unfailingly find his way to his own family.

On account of its exact adaptability to prairie life, the tipi was taken as the model of the army tent which bears the name of General Sibley and is now used by our army.

HOW INDIANS MADE PAINTS

Indians in old times used a great many different colors for various purposes. They valued highly these coloring materials, and in intertribal commerce they traded valuable goods in exchange for them. These dyes and paints were of immemorial manufacture and use among Indians. A Dakota told me that he did not know all the pigments, but he could tell about some of them. He said he could tell something about paints made from different earths. He said his people, the Dakotas, used to make a white powder for whitening hides, and color paints, as brown, yellow, and blue. The raw material for these commodities was obtained by the Dakotas from natural deposits, usually in certain banks, either river banks or bluffs. In various deposits in different places they obtained clays of different colors. They gave local names to these places, and so in talking about them at any time they could identify the places and say they got clay for blue paint at such a place, and clay for yellow paint at such and such a place, and so on. They knew where all these places were and were acquainted with the names of the places and the product found at each.

To prepare the paints, the different clays were baked over a fire. The baking changed the color of the clay, besides driving out moisture. The paint makers knew which clay would be changed to red, which to yellow, and which to brown, and so forth. After the clays were baked, they were finely pulverized in a mortar and then packed away in buckskin bags for preservation or transport. Whenever the paint was to be used, a portion would be measured out and thoroughly mixed with tallow, being kneaded and worked in the palm of the hand.

One of the colors was a brownish red like the darkest red pipestone. This was used on the faces and hands of little children as a remedy for eczema or any eruption of the skin, and as a protection for the skin in frosty weather. When applied, it caused the persons to appear of a dark red color.

Blue clay for paint was found in banks in certain places, and was prepared and used commonly in various ways. The whiting which was used to make hides white was made from a shining white stone which is found in pieces scattered more or less abundantly in certain places. This shining white stone is what we call selenite. When heated, it becomes a fine white powder. This powder was used for whitening buckskin, and also for whitening the skin tipis. After tent skins had been whitened, they were decorated with designs laid on in the dark red and black paints.

Nowadays the Dakotas use for the most part paints and dyes made by white men. Before white men came, the Dakotas, it is said, made paints and dyes mainly for their own use, not for purposes of trade.

THE WONDERFUL BASKET

Indians of all tribes held the thought of the brotherhood of all living nature—of the trees and flowers and grasses, of the fishes in the waters, of the living things which creep or walk or run on the land, of the birds which fly above the earth, and of human beings. And they believed that human beings often gained wisdom and useful information through dreams and visions in which the guardian spirits of any of these other living creatures talked to them, revealing to chosen, attentive and worthy persons secrets of nature which were hidden from the careless and unworthy.

Among most tribes the cedar tree is considered to possess a property of mystery and sacredness. For this reason, twigs of cedar were often burned as incense in a sacred fire to drive away evil influences. And if a person reclined under the shelter of cedar trees, the healing power and strength of their spirit would come to him, and his own spirit would thus gain composure and strength to meet life's troubles.

Once in the old times a Mandan woman was resting under a cedar tree. She was weary from her work, and as the gentle wind sighed among the thick green branches above her, she dropped to sleep. While she slept, the cedar tree spoke to her in a soft murmuring voice, and the woman gave heed to the words of the cedar tree.

And this is what the cedar tree said to the woman: "Sister, if you will dig down into the earth, you will find there my slender, strong, pliant roots. Take up some of these and weave them into a basket. You will find thereafter that some good shall come of it. It shall bring good to you and to all women."

So the woman did as she was told by the cedar tree. She took up the slender roots and wove of them a basket. The basket was light but strong, and so pliant that it could be rolled into a small bundle when empty, though it was large enough to hold many things when it was opened out.

One day the woman took the basket with her and walked far out upon the prairie where tipsin grew in abundance. She dug a quantity of the sweet and wholesome roots to take home for food for herself and her family. The tipsin roots grow so deep in the tough prairie sod that it is hard work to dig them, and so when she had filled her basket she was very tired. She sat down to rest and sighed for very weariness, and the tears came to her eyes. She said, "Alas! Now I must carry home this heavy load, although I am already weary and faint."

Then the basket whispered to her: "Do not cry. Wipe away your tears; bathe your hot cheeks with water at the brook; be glad, for I am your friend."

Then the woman wiped away her tears and went and bathed her cheeks and brushed her hair. When she returned, the basket seemed to smile. It said to her: "You were troubled for nothing. You forget what the cedar tree said to you in your dreams. You were told that good would come to you if you made a basket as you were instructed. Now you need not carry your load; but sing and be glad and walk on to the village. I shall come with you, carrying your load."

So the woman went on her way home, singing from happiness, while the basket kept by her side carrying the load of tipsin roots.

As she came near the village, the women knew by her happy singing voice that some good thing had happened to her. Then as they looked up they saw her coming, and with her was coming the wonderful basket carrying the load.

Then all her neighbors begged her to teach them

how to make a wonderful basket. So she taught them, as she had been taught by the holy cedar tree, how to make a wonderful basket out of its tiny roots.

And so, from that time, whenever a woman went out to gather June berries or wild cherries or raspberries or wild plums or pembinas or tipsin or wild rice, or went to the cultivated fields to gather corn or beans, she was not obliged to carry the load home. When she was ready, she started toward the village singing, and the basket came with her, cheerfully carrying the burden.

One day, long after this, a woman found the winter storehouse of the bean mouse people, which they make underground, and into which they garner their store of food for the winter time. The hard-working bean mouse people put away in their storehouses quantities of wild ground beans and various kinds of seeds and roots and tubers to provide themselves food for the cold time when the ground is frozen and the earth is covered with snow.

It happened that the woman who found this storehouse of the bean mouse people was one who was not considerate of the rights of others. She thought only that here was a quantity of food which was desirable and easy to obtain. So she filled her basket with the wild ground beans, which are so delicious when cooked with bits of meat. She cared not that it had cost the bean mouse people many weary hours of hard work to dig these beans and bring them together in this place, nor did she care that without

them the bean mouse people, their old people and
their little ones, all would be left destitute of food
and must perish from famine.

While she was filling her basket, a poor little bean
mouse woman cried pitifully and said: "This is our
food. We have worked hard for it. You ought not
to rob us of it. Without it we shall die miserably of
hunger." But the woman took the beans and heeded
not the pitiful crying of the bean mouse woman.
She had filled her basket and was making ready to
go home, but there was no song in her heart.

Then, while the filled basket sat there waiting, a
coyote came near and laughed. At this the basket
was vexed and said: "You are rude. Why do you
laugh at me?" But the coyote only laughed all the
more. This annoyed the basket greatly, and made
it feel very uneasy and distressed, for it knew something must be wrong. And it said to the coyote:
"Do tell me why you laugh. What is it that is
strange?"

Then the coyote replied: "I laugh because you are
so foolish. For a long time you have been carrying
burdens to the village while the women go their
way singing."

But the basket said: "I am not foolish; I have
the good spirit of the cedar tree. I am willing to
carry burdens to help the women. I am glad when
I hear their joyful singing."

The coyote said: "But what do you get for it,
friend? You work like a slave. You receive noth-

ing for it. No one offers you a mouthful of food.
When you rest for a time from your labor, you are
not covered with a robe made beautiful with quillwork. When you have carried burdens for a woman, she merely hangs you upon a peg on the wall
till the next time she wishes you to carry something
for her."

As the basket considered the things which the
coyote said, it began to be discontented. It felt that
it had been treated unfairly, that it had no pay nor
thanks for all it had done; and so the basket was
sulky and refused to carry the load to the village,
and the woman at last had to take up the burden and
carry it upon her back; and she felt aggrieved and
bitter because the basket would not carry it for her.
She did not consider that all the service she had ever
had from the basket was from kindness and good
will and not from obligation.

And ever since that time the women have had to
carry burdens upon their backs, for the baskets no
longer carried burdens for them.

AN OMAHA GHOST STORY

In the springtime a little child had died and was
buried on the hill southeast of the village. The hill
was green with the prairie grass and spangled with
the beautiful wild flowers of the prairie. On the
north and east the forest ascends the slope from the
Missouri River valley to the crest of the hill, partly

encircling the burial place with a rampart of green trees in which were numbers of happy birds, busy with their nest-building and tuneful with their joyful songs.

Not long after the death of this little child, the people went upon the annual summer buffalo hunt to the Sand Hill region many miles away to the west from the village. As the people drew away from the familiar home scenes of the village, the mother was strongly affected by a feeling of sadness and grief for her little one whom she had to leave alone in its narrow bed upon the hill. When the people had made camp and the evening meal was prepared, this mother was so burdened with grief for her child that she could not eat and went away to grieve alone. When she left the camp, she was so drawn by yearning for her little one that she walked on and on all night toward the home village. In the morning, weak and weary, she was back in the deserted village. All was still. Not a person and not a dog was there. She went into her own house. Then she went through the village to other houses. At some deserted fireplace she happened to find some coals; so she was able to kindle a fire and cook a bit of food. She sat in her house and wailed for her baby. After a time she heard sounds. She listened, and there seemed to be whispers and murmurs all about her. And so it continued day after day. At first she saw nothing, but heard the murmurs and whispers, and gradually she could almost understand what the

whispers said, especially when she fasted. She made
out enough to know that it was the spirits of the
departed, who, in the absence of the living, returned
to occupy the houses.

After a time she became able to understand more
of what the ghosts said, and finally she could talk
with them in their own manner. Their speech was
not like the speech of living people; there was no
voice, but there were slight whispering sounds, such
as one sometimes hears among the grass on the
prairie when all is still, or among the leaves of
growing corn, or among the cottonwood leaves on a
quiet evening.

At first the woman saw nothing, though she could
hear the whispering speech like the breathing of
those who sleep. Later she could see, as it seemed,
feet moving about on the floor, but nothing above
the feet. As she looked, she could see nothing between herself and the opposite walls of the house.
Then, after a time, she seemed to see not only the
moccasins but the leggings above them as far as the
knees, but she never saw any more. And thus it
was with her during all the time she dwelt there
alone with the spirits, until her people returned to
the village.

This time it happened that the people did not return for a year. When the woman had disappeared
from the camp on their first night out, the people
supposed she had gone out somewhere to be alone
to weep and pray; but when she did not return, they

sought for her, and not being able to find any trace of her, they supposed that some accident had befallen her and that she was dead. They were much surprised to find her at home when they returned to the village at the end of a year. But when they spoke to her, they found that she was mute; she moved her lips, but no sound came. After some days she recovered speech and again took up her accustomed life with her people.

During the year in which she lived alone in the deserted village, she had planted and harvested a crop and had lived by that, by what food had been left in the storage places, and by the wild products which she gathered.

PERSONAL NAMES AMONG INDIANS

There seems to be much error and misunderstanding among white people concerning personal names among Indians. We often hear very strange and curious statements made in that regard. For a proper understanding of the subject of names, both personal and family, we should consider the fact that the origin of names is similar in fundamental purpose and significance among all the peoples of the earth, differing only in superficial details. Two very common sources of personal names among all peoples everywhere in all time have been the invocation of aid and guardianship of supernatural powers and the commemoration of notable events.

Familiar examples of these sources of personal names are to be found in most of the old Hebrew names in the Bible. And with the adoption of Christianity by various nations, these old Hebrew names have been adopted also among all nations. So we have such names as Isaac, Jacob, Joseph, Emmanuel, David, and so forth.

White people very often say that Indian names are strange. This notion commonly comes from the insistence that Indian names be translated so that their meaning shall be apparent, although neither our own names nor the names of other nationalities who come among us are so translated. Sometimes the Indian names have been fairly well translated, but again many have been grossly mistranslated, and thus have been made to appear grotesque. Even when correctly translated, they often appear strange to our people because in their proper meanings they contain allusions to manners and customs which, common as they may have been among the people where they originated, are unknown among our people. But then we should consider that their customs are no more strange to us than ours would be to them.

Perhaps if all our names were translated into English, many of them also would sound strange. Our people are of many national origins, and so our names have come from many languages. Sometimes these names have come from our ancestral racial origin, as Gaelic, Germanic, Slavic, or what not;

sometimes they have come from the cultural origins of our civilization, as Hebrew, Greek, and Roman.

Perhaps the translation of some of our common names into English will make my meaning plain. To be sure, we have some common names that are simply English words, whose meanings are plain enough when we stop to think of them. Thus we have the masculine name Ernest, the feminine names Lily, Rose, Charity, Faith, Patience, Hope, Prudence, Delight, Joy, and so forth. From the Greek we have such names as George, Philip, Theodore and its feminine forms Theodora and Dorothea and Dorothy; from the Germanic, the names Gottlieb, Sigrid, Herbert, Alfhild, Alfred, and so forth. The Slavic name Bohumil has the same meaning as the Germanic name Gottlieb. Now let us translate these and see if they do not look as strange as Indian names when they are translated: George—Worker-of-the-earth, or Farmer; Philip —Lover-of-horses; Theodore (and its feminine forms)—Gift-of-God; Gottlieb—God-love; Sigrid —Council-of-victory; Herbert —Glory-of-the-army; Alfhild—Heroine-of-the-elves; Alfred— Council-of-the-elves. The Slavic Vladimir means Lord-of-the-world. There is an old Gaelic (Irish) name which, translated into English, would be Chief -who-gets-them-up-early-in-the-morning. Of Gaelic origin we have the names Gilchrist, Gilmore, Gilroy, Gillivray, MacNamara, and many others. Gilchrist is a corruption on the English tongue of the

Gaelic name, Giolla-Christ, meaning Follower-of-Christ. Gilmore and all its variations—Gilmour, Gilmer, Gilmary, and Gilmurry—are corruptions on the English tongue of the Gaelic name Giolla-Muire, which means Devotee-of-Mary, Muire or Mary being the mother of Jesus. The name Gilroy is an English corruption of a Gaelic name which means Red-fellow, referring to the complexion and color of the hair. Gillivray is an English corruption of a Gaelic name which means Freckle-faced-fellow. The name MacNamara is a corruption on the English tongue of the old Gaelic name Mac-con-na-Mara, which means Son-of-the-hero-of-the-Sea. By these examples of some of our names you will see that Indian names are not so different from our names after all, when we examine their meanings.

Among Indians of all the tribes of my acquaintance there are three main sources of personal names. First, there is a list of names which are common in the tribe, which names have come down for a long time from generation to generation. Second, there are names which relate to visions or divine visitations obtained, usually, by some relative of the person on whom such a name was bestowed. Third, there are names which are in themselves tokens of achievement, of accomplishment of worthy deeds, of dignity and worth in the individuals on whom they were conferred. In all cases the personal name, among Indians, is considered a part of the character and personality of the individual possessing it. Personal names are conferred upon individuals by appropriate dignified public ceremony. The conferring of a name upon a person is a priestly function.

Names of the first two classes mentioned are conferred in childhood. Names of the third class— that is, achievement names—are conferred upon adults at any time of life, in recognition of the performance of deeds of special valor or of other notable and worthy achievements or public services. When a new name is thus attained by anyone, his former name is dropped; he is thenceforth known by the new name alone.

The naming ceremony is conducted with religious ritual. In Indian religious thought, the universe is conceived as a living, unified community in which all living things, plants as well as animals and men, from the lowest and most humble to the highest and proudest, the spirit beings, and all the elements and powers of the earth and heaven, have their proper and useful places. Man, as one of the forms of living beings in this universal community, is in vital relation with all others. So when a man is given a name it is done publicly, and ritualistic proclamation is made to all the Powers and all other living things in all four quarters of the universe, to Mother Earth and to the Supreme Power, the Chief Above. When a name of the third class, a name from personal achievement is conferred on a man, it is thus publicly proclaimed to be known of all: to the Sunrise, the source of life and light and energy; to the Water, the sustainer of all life—the waters of the clouds and the dew, the waters of streams and lakes; to the Winds, which give movement and breath of life to all things; to Night, which brings rest and restoration to all things; to all vegetation, which beautifies and enriches the earth—to the trees and grasses and flowers which gladden the eyes of man, to the nut trees and fruit trees and all other plants which bring gifts of food and medicine and perfume and other gifts for the comfort and delight of man; to the animals which move about on the earth and in its waters; to the birds and all creatures great and small which fly about in the air; to all these fellow creatures of man in the universe it is proclaimed that the person here present is now no longer to be known by the name which was his formerly, but is henceforth to be known by the new name. And with this it is also proclaimed that the new name is given in recognition of the worthy deeds or achievements cited.

Nicknames are very frequently attached among Indians on account of some striking event or from some personal peculiarity. Such nicknames commonly are acquired among Indians in their ordinary association with each other, and also frequently nicknames are applied to white men with whom they have come in contact. Thus Captain Clark, of the Lewis and Clark expedition, was nicknamed "Red-hair" among the Indian tribes, because of a physical characteristic. General Nelson A. Miles once made a winter campaign against Indians in Montana. Because of the severe cold, he wore a bearskin overcoat. From this circumstance the Indians nicknamed him "Bear-coat." And he has been known by that designation ever since among the Indians of that region.

These nicknames, whether of Indians or applied by them to white men, are not at all regarded in the same mental attitude as real names. They are nowise considered as linking the person with the mystic and spiritual world, as are the real names.

Perhaps I can best show the significance of a personal name in an Indian tribe, and of its conferment, by relating the circumstance of my own acquirement of a personal name in the Skidi tribe of the Pawnee nation. I need not here go into the reasons for which the honor was bestowed upon me. I need only say that one day Letekats-taka, who was chief of the Skidis, said to me, "My friend, I have in mind to give you a Pawnee name." Of course I felt honored and gratified. He continued, "I have two names in mind. I have not yet decided which name I shall confer upon you." Then he told me the two names he was considering. One was the name of a noted hero of their tribe who had lived long ago. The other was the name of a certain hill, the most noted place in all the Pawnee country. The name of this hill is Pahok. This hill is the chief mythic place of all the mythic places in the Pawnee my-

thology. We might say Pahok was to the Pawnees
what Mount Olympus was to the Greeks, or what
Mount Zion was to the Hebrews. The story of the
hill called Pahok is told elsewhere in this book.

In nature and appearance, Pahok is quite different
from any other hill in the vicinity. It dominates
all the landscape as far as one can see. It has
an appearance of strength and of serene and un-
perturbed calm. It stands facing northwest in a
curve of the wide stream of the Platte River. Before it, on the opposite side of the river, the level
prairie in the broad valley stretches away for many
miles. From the opposite shore, Pahok, with the
river sweeping in a wide curve about its foot, appears,
as the Indians say, "like a mountain island rising out
of the water." The meaning of the Pawnee word
pahok is "headland" or "promontory." And now
it will be seen why the Pawnees called this hill The
Headland or The Promontory.

The front of Pahok is dark with a heavy growth
of timber. This adds to the air of mystery and
grandeur which clothes The Promontory, the more
so as among the timber are many solemn red cedars,
a tree which to the Indians has a character of mystery and holiness. The Promontory stands there
with an appearance of ponderous meditation, gazing
out sphynx-like across the expanse of water and of
level land, while on each side to the rear the lower
prairie hills range away, seeming to repose in the
calm strength of The Promontory.

The old man, Chief Letekats-taka, was meditating. At last he looked up and spoke. He said, "My friend, I have decided. I shall proclaim that you are to be known henceforth among Pawnees as Pahok." Of course I was filled with feelings of gratitude and pride, but also of humility, when I thought of the meaning of it and recalled the story of the myth of this noted place. I said, "But, my friend, the young man in the story of Pahok did wonderful things for his people." The old man smiled and said to me, "You also do wonderful things."

To be sure, I prized the name at the time it was conferred upon me, but I have appreciated it still more highly in the years since then, and the more as I have come to sense the high esteem in which it is regarded by the Indians. Sometimes this regard has even been mentioned, and Indians have said to me, "That is a good name you have; a very honorable name."

FALSE NOTIONS ABOUT INDIANS

There are many false notions and erroneous ideas about Indians current everywhere. Our people should be better informed. To have any proper estimate and understanding of the native race of America—the Indians, so called—we must clear away some of this great mass of misinformation.

One of the most common errors is that all Indians are one people, of one language and of similar habits all over the continent. This is far from true. On the contrary, there are more than fifty distinctly different racial stocks in North America north of Mexico. These different racial stocks are divided each into several different tribes and nations, each with its own language, so that we find more than two hundred Indian languages within the limits of the United States and Canada, to say nothing of the number of dialects of each distinct language. Altogether there might well be several hundred dialects, for there are sometimes several dialects in one language: thus the Dakota language has four or five dialects, and there are several dialects of each other language of the Siouan group. In the Caddoan group there are also several different dialects of each language: for example, the Pawnee language, which is one of the Caddoan group, has several dialects. It should therefore be well remembered that to say "the Indian language" has no more meaning or sense than to say "the white language," which everyone knows would have no meaning at all, for there are many white languages. So also there are very many Indian languages.

And as the different tribes and nations of Indians differ in language, so do they also differ in customs, manners, and habits of living. These all differ according to the differences of geographic conditions and the natural resources of the different regions of the continent. The different tribes and nations of Indians differ from each other also in physical appearance and features, just as white nations do. Everyone knows, for example, that Swedes, Scots, Germans and Italians differ very much in looks. Just as much do Dakotas, Pawnees, Osages and others differ from each other in looks.

Another popular error in regard to Indians is that they had no fixed places of abode, but were nomads and wanderers. A common saying is that certain tribes "roamed over the prairie," or that certain other tribes "wandered in the forest." Indians of all tribes traveled, just as white men travel, for definite purposes. But all Indian nations had their own territories or countries. And these different Indian countries were marked from each other by known boundary lines determined by intertribal treaties. Within their own countries, the various tribes and nations had their fixed villages and towns, made up of permanent houses, clustered near together for social and economic reasons. Near these towns they had their fields of cultivated crops.

Another error is that Indians always had ponies. The fact is that there were no horses of any kind in the western hemisphere until they were brought over by the Spaniards.

There is a popular error in regard to the subsistence of Indians. White people commonly think of Indians as meat-eaters mainly. The fact is that a very considerable part of the diet of Indians was of vegetable origin—seeds, fruits, roots, tubers, nuts, and other plant products.

It is also commonly held that Indians are very taciturn, lacking in any sense of humor or enjoyment of fun. It is even said that Indians are sullen. But this is not true. I do not know any race more fun-loving and merry, or with a keener sense of humor. And a more truly sociable people than Indians, of all the tribes with which I am acquainted, I never have known.

Origin
& Distribution
of
Aboriginal
Agriculture
—
North
America

(X) Supposed center of original
domestication of corn.

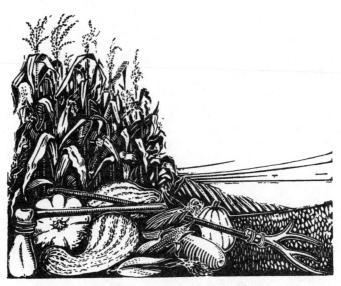

THE TRIBES OF MEN

EARLY INDIAN AGRICULTURE

Most people of this country, of the now dominant European race, seldom give a thought to the economic conditions which prevailed here before this country was Europeanized. They seldom think of the pre-Columbian utilization of the natural resources of this continent by the people of the native American race. They do not consider the myriad uses of plants and plant products by the people of the native tribes. Most persons of our European race, in arrogant self-satisfaction, have not been accustomed to think of those of the American race as agriculturists at all; much less have we given thought to the contributions made by that race to the world's agriculture.

No doubt the beginning of agriculture, with our own European race and with every race, was simply the gathering and storing of supplies of wild plant products; and no doubt agriculture proceeded by the stages of intentional dissemination, cultivation, selection, and improvement of stock into myriad varieties.

When European explorers first visited the Atlantic shores of America, they found the native tribes to be agriculturists, living in villages of permanent houses, and with their cultivated fields stretching about the villages. And as the explorers advanced into the interior of the continent they found similar conditions to prevail as far as to and including the Missouri River valley. So it was found that in all the region from the Gulf of Mexico to the St. Lawrence River, the Great Lakes, and the region of the upper Missouri River all the various Indian nations were settled agriculturists. On the high plains and in the western mountains the tribes could not cultivate the soil because of the unfavorable conditions.

The crops cultivated by the tribes in the region above defined consisted of corn, beans, squashes and pumpkins in many varieties, gourds, sunflowers, "Jerusalem artichokes," and tobacco. The sunflower is native to the western and southern plains and was there brought under cultivation and improved to what we have as the cultivated sunflower and was distributed throughout the region from the Great Plains to the Atlantic coast. The other crops above named were introduced from the south many centuries ago—from Mexico. Their wild ancestors grow there, which would indicate that there they were first brought into domestication by cultivation and improvement of the wild stock. All evidence from every source seems to point to the plateau of southeast Mexico or Yucatan as the place of origin of corn. It seems to have been originally a large, coarse wild grass with seeds which were at least large enough to furnish an article of food when gathered in quantity. The botanical evidence would indicate that it had a branched stalk and that all the branches and the terminal alike bore loose panicles of seeds, not seeds in compact ears like the corn ear that we now know. Ages of cultivation and selection by obscure and forgotten tribes of primitive farmers have produced a plant which bears its staminate flowers generally on the terminal and its pistillate flowers on side branches modified into what we know as corn ears. Not only had the above-described modification taken place in the process of long ages of cultivation and selection, but the five great types of corn had been formed and developed into innumerable varieties of each type prior to the advent of white men on this continent. The five types to which I have referred are dent corn, flour corn, flint corn, sweet corn, and pop corn. Dent corn was obtained first by white men from the Indians of Virginia in the beginning of the seventeenth century at the first settlement of that colony by the English. The New England tribes had flint corn, flour corn, and sweet corn, and probably pop corn, but not dent corn. The tribes of the upper Missouri River had flint corn, flour corn, and sweet corn.

The Arikaras and Mandans on the upper Missouri were the great agricultural tribes of their region. Omaha legend credits the Arikaras with first having corn and with having distributed it to other tribes. And the common pictograph to represent the Arikaras among all the surrounding tribes was a conventionalized ear of corn. In the sign language also, the surrounding tribes designated the Arikaras by a motion of the hands depicting the act of shelling corn, or by the motions of eating an ear of corn. Washington Matthews says: "There are some reasons for believing that the Arikara represent an older race of farmers than the Mandan; for their religious ceremonies connected with the planting are the more numerous, and they honor the corn with a species of worship." And it is the work of these northern tribes in past centuries in acclimating corn to the short northern summer with its cool nights which has made it possible for the states of North Dakota, Montana and Minnesota now to be corn-producing states; for acclimation is a long and gradual process, and the acclimation of corn was accomplished during a northward migration from Mexico which occupied many centuries of time.

In the arid region of what is now New Mexico and Arizona, the work of agriculture was carried on by means of irrigation ages before the coming of white men, and the old irrigation ditches made by the primitive Indian farmers of that region may still be traced—irrigation works made without other power than human muscles and without the use of iron, the shovels used being made of bone, stone and wood.

The world is indebted to the aboriginal American agriculturists not only for all types of corn which we now have, but also beans, pumpkins and squashes, cultivated sunflowers, sweet potatoes, peanuts, and many other crops among our present-day staples.

A great handicap to primitive American farmers was the lack of iron tools; for they had no iron before the coming of white men. Another handicap was the absence of horses. The horse was not native to the western hemisphere, and was first introduced by the Spaniards. Previously the only beast of burden in North America was the dog. So the cultivation of the ground was entirely handwork; and the tool most in use was a hoe made from the shoulder blade of the buffalo or of the elk. One may imagine the immense labor which was required to develop and extend the above-named crops over the continent, acclimated and ready to our hands when we arrived in the New World.

TRADING BETWEEN TRIBES

In aboriginal times the course of the Missouri River formed one of the main lines of intertribal commerce between north and south, and along its tributaries were crosslines between east and west. Fixed routes of travel, known and used by the tribes for many centuries before the coming of white men, lay along these watercourses. Streams determined the lines of travel, because water for drinking and cooking and wood for fuel were prime necessities. In the prairie country, wood was found growing only along the courses of the streams. By means of these great travel ways, there was much interchange of natural products from mountains and valleys, from prairies and forests, between peoples of regions greatly differing in their mineral and plant and animal resources. There was much interchange of all these material things, but there was also much interchange of ideas, of stories, of poetic and mythologic conceptions, of knowledge of the Indians' world, its geography and natural resources, of the habits and customs of distant tribes and nations, and of the arts and crafts of different racial stocks and cultural inheritances. All this interchange made for the enrichment of life.

The Arikara nation on the upper Missouri River was of the Caddoan stock. The Arikaras and the related nation, the Pawnees, were the foremost in culture among all the tribes of the prairie countries.

They were the pioneers in agriculture in all that region, and had been the teachers of the art and science of agriculture to all the other tribes of that region which practiced it. They had also taught them the Caddoan architecture, pottery, and other arts. The products of Caddoan agriculture were eagerly sought by the tribes dwelling on the high plains to the west of them, and in the Rocky Mountains beyond, in neither of which regions could agriculture be carried on.

At the time of green-corn harvest, the agricultural tribes along the Missouri River were sure to have many visitors from the plains tribes. These tribes noted the time of appearance of the blossoms of a prairie flower commonly called "the blazing star." When this flower came into bloom they would say: "Now the corn of the Arikaras is coming into condition for eating. Let us go and visit them." So they resorted to the villages of the Arikaras, bringing with them the products of the natural resources of their own countries and the products of their own handicraft as presents and as commodities of trade. At this time in summer, and again in the fall, when the ripe corn, beans, squashes, and sunflower seeds were harvested, the people of distant tribes came to the Arikaras and other agricultural tribes, and for many days engaged in mutual exchange of commodities.

The most common unit of measure of volume of commodities among the Arikaras was the *hunansadu*, the measure of the contents of the common burden basket, the capacity of which was a little less than the English bushel. One *hunansadu* of shelled corn was considered equal in value to one good buffalo robe or two packs of dried meat. A meat pack was two cubits in length, one cubit wide, and one cubit thick.

One of the most common commodities brought by the western Dakotas to trade to the Arikaras was dried tipsin roots. This plant belongs to the bean family, but it is not its seeds which are used. The root of the tipsin is a single tap root, the upper part enlarged with stored food till it is about the size of a hen's egg. It is what was called *pomme blanche* by the early French trappers. The enlarged roots of tipsin formed a staple food product of the prairie. It was eaten cooked when fresh, and was also dried in great quantity to preserve it for future use. Commonly the roots were peeled and braided together by the pliant fibrous root tips, as ears of corn are braided together by the turned-back husks. They were also split and dried loose. When dried loose in this way, they were measured by the *hunansadu;* when braided together, the strings were made of a standard length, namely, one arm-reach. One arm-reach was the length from the breastbone along the outstretched arm to the finger tips. One *hunansadu* of shelled corn was valued at four strings of tipsin roots or one *hunansadu* of split roots of tipsin.

Dried native wild fruits, such as the chokecherry

and the June berry, were also articles of intertribal commerce. The agricultural tribes prepared some of these for themselves, but being occupied with the care of their cultivated crops they did not put up such great quantities of them as did the non-agricultural tribes on the high plains. Consequently the agricultural tribes traded surplus products of their crops for the surplus products of the non-agricultural tribes. When the Arikaras traded with the Dakotas, they paid one *hunansadu* of shelled corn for one-half *hunansadu* of dried chokecherries. When they bought dried June berries, they paid for them at the same rate as for chokecherries. June berries are harder to gather than chokecherries, but easier to prepare by drying. The chokecherries are easy to gather, but the process of pounding them to a pulp, shaping this pulp into cakes and drying them is laborious; hence they were equal in price.

The unit measure for squash strung and dried was one double arm-reach—that is, the distance between the finger tips of the two hands outstretched horizontally. The Dakotas would receive four strings of dried squash for one plain buffalo robe, nicely tanned. Of course a decorated robe, painted or embroidered with porcupine quill work, brought a proportionately higher price. Four strings of dried squash would also be the price for three packs of dried meat. The volume of a meat pack has already been defined.

The Crees and the Chippewas from the woodland

to the eastward also came to the tribes on the Missouri River to trade. They brought the dried meat of the moose and furs and skins of smaller animals which were to be found in their woodland country but not in the prairie country. The Chippewas also brought maple sugar. Various other products of the woodland were brought by these tribes, and these products were in demand by Missouri River tribes and also by their customers from the high plains and the Rocky Mountains. Articles which the mountain tribes had obtained from other tribes still farther west were thus brought by them to the Missouri River, and in turn might be bought by Crees or Chippewas and carried back beyond the Red River of the North into the woodland region around the Great Lakes. In this way commodities often were carried in trade for long distances: dentalium shells from the Pacific coast, certain plant products from Montana, and other plant products from Arizona, far away to the south, were thus imported into the region of the Missouri River.

There are no salt springs or deposits of rock salt in the country of the Arikaras; and because of its weight and the difficulties of transportation, this commodity was scarce and very dear among the Arikaras. However, small quantities were imported from the country of the Otos and from the Kansas, five hundred miles away to the south.

The best of all woods for bow-making is the Osage orange, called by the French *bois d'arc*, which means "bow-wood." This wood is native in south-eastern Oklahoma and southwestern Arkansas, a thousand miles away to the south from the Arikara country. Bows made of this wood were in great demand, and the price of one among the Arikaras was one horse and one blanket.

From the southern plains the Cheyennes brought plant and mineral products of their country, and also horses, to trade with the people of the Missouri River for their agricultural products, and for the commodities which they had in turn obtained from other distant tribes.

The Assiniboines came down from the north bringing the commodities from their own country, and also commodities that they had obtained from other tribes still farther to the north. So the villages of the Missouri River tribes were great trading stations and ports of exchange for the diverse products of regions of great extent, and in this respect resembled the great market towns on the caravan routes of central Asia.

INDIAN IDEAS OF PROPERTY

The aboriginal Indian ideas of property rights differed from those held by white men, and so were the frequent cause of misunderstanding and war between the races. For instance, white men have commonly held to the theory of individual property in land, and the right of an individual to negotiate the purchase or the sale of land as property. Such an idea as this was entirely alien to the Indian mind. Therefore the common saying that the island of Manhattan was "purchased from its Indian inhabitants for the value of twenty-four dollars in traders' goods" is not true. It is not true for the reason that the Indians did not and could not think of the possibility of conveying property in land. What the Indians of Manhattan did conceive was the idea of admitting the Dutch settlers to live in the land with themselves as neighbors, to share its benefits. But they had no idea of selling the land for any price. No Indians of Manhattan or elsewhere entertained at any time any such idea. Indians always said in opposition to such proposals, "We cannot sell the land, for it belongs not to us in this generation only, but to all our people for all time, to our children and our children's children as much as to us, and we cannot sell what is theirs." When the Indians of Manhattan Island accepted goods from the Dutch at the time of the agreement to permit them to live there as their neighbors, it was not with any thought of accepting a purchase price for the land. They thought of the goods given by the Dutch as being merely presents given as a pledge and token of good will and neighborly relations. The idea of alienation of the land was never in their minds.

I wish to say something about Indian ideas of family leasehold of land within the tribal domain, under the common law of the tribe, for the purpose of house site and the tillage of crops. What I have to say is from personal knowledge and acquaintance with the tribes I know best, those of the Missouri River region—the Pawnee, Omaha, Oto, Ponka, Dakota, Arikara, Mandan and Hidatsa nations. I will also say something in regard to popular vested rights in the benefits of natural resources, even those within the domain of some other tribe. These were matters of intertribal reciprocal courtesy and custom. It was felt that all things necessary to human life and comfort should be accessible to all people and should be monopolized by none to the exclusion of any others.

In this category are to be included all useful mineral resources, temporary resort to mineral waters and thermal springs for curative purposes, the right to gather plant products for alimental, medicinal, cosmetic, manufacturing, dyeing, and other uses, and the taking of game animals and fish.

For example, some mineral products were found in the Pawnee country which were not in the Omaha country. Some other minerals were found in the Omaha country which were not in the country of the Pawnees nor of the Otos. Still others were in the country of the Otos and not in either the Pawnee or the Omaha country. Likewise, certain useful plant products abounded in the country of one or other of the tribes and were scanty or absent in the territories of other tribes. Like conditions existed with regard to certain animal resources. In such cases reciprocal privileges were mutually allowed.

The slaughter of the buffalo was not an individual enterprise, but a corporate community industry, carried on under strict police regulations according to tribal laws. Any infraction of these regulations was strictly and severely punished. The regular buffalo hunt was a community expedition under the lead and control of responsible officers. Under the direction of these officers, all persons taking part in the expedition were assigned their several stations in the various parts of the work of slaughter and of preparation of the meat and other products. And the final distribution of the meat, skins, and other products was made according to equitable regulations fixed by law.

The grazing habits of the buffaloes, feeding together as they did in very large herds, caused them to range over areas hundreds of miles in extent, moving across intertribal boundary lines. Thus by the movement of the herds a tribe might sometimes be deprived of any opportunity to obtain the meat and other products of the buffalo which were so necessary to them for sustenance. The case might be that the buffaloes had all gone out of the Omaha country and over into the country of the Pawnees. In such a case the Omaha officers applied to the authorities of the Pawnee nation and received permission to follow the herds into the Pawnee country, and submitted themselves to the direction of the

Pawnee officers of the hunt, according to the regulations of Pawnee law. On the other hand, if a Pawnee party went into the Omaha country, it submitted to Omaha regulations and to Omaha officers.

In the Oto country, near the site of the present city of Lincoln, there was a salt marsh from which, in the dry season, salt was obtained not only by the Oto people but also by the people of the neighboring tribes, the Omaha and the Pawnee. In the Kansas country also, there were good deposits of salt. But the Kansas had no thought of interposing any objection to their neighbors, the Pawnee and other tribes, resorting thither to take salt.

In the country of the Ponkas was a deposit of a ferruginous shale which was used as one of the ingredients in making a black dye. The Ponkas freely permitted their neighbors, the Omahas and Pawnees, and any others who wished, to take shale from this deposit.

The famous catlinite quarry is in the country of the Santee Dakotas, the eastern tribe of the Dakota nation, but expeditions from many other tribes within a radius of hundreds of miles resorted to it without hindrance from the Dakotas, in order to obtain the material from which to make their ceremonial pipes.

And thus it was with the deposits of selenite in the southern part of the Pawnee country, the deposits of pure kaolin in the southwestern part of the country of the Teton Dakotas, the antiphlogistic earth found in the country of a tribe in what is now eastern Colorado, deposits of flint, of pottery clay, and so forth, in various places. All such deposits were freely accessible to working parties from other tribes, who could take what they required for their needs.

Tenure of parcels of tribal land by individuals and groups within a tribe was determined by preemption and occupancy in use. Such a parcel of ground might be held as the site of a dwelling, as a field for growing crops, or as a burial site.

All the tribes lived in village communities. According to its population, a tribe contained one or more villages. In laying out a village after a complete removal, or in founding a new village as a colony from a village already established, the heads of families chose the sites upon which their several dwellings were to be erected within the limits determined by the committee on location as to the bounds of the village. After the location of dwelling sites, the next act was the choice of fields and garden sites. Preëmption of such a site was indicated by a claimant's marking out its bounds by stakes, stones or earth mounds. A claimant's boundary marks were respected by all others. In case of a dispute, opposing claimants submitted their case to arbitration and abode peaceably by the decision of the arbiters. It was held that contentious dispute about landholdings would always bring ill fortune to both parties to the controversy, because the land is holy, and any selfish contention in regard to a holy thing would bring nothing but evil results. So the people religiously abstained from any quarreling over land, and no one would think of trying to seize a piece of land occupied by another. Such impiety, they felt sure, would entail severe and proper punishment. I find this idea commonly prevalent among the several tribes of my acquaintance. The Hidatsas have a story bearing upon this principle. The story tells of a black bear which took possession of another bear's den. The punishment which fell upon the aggressor was that he became crazy.

When an individual or a family had set up title to hold a piece of ground for planting, it was an undisputed possession so long as that individual maintained the use of it. If a piece of ground was abandoned by its tenant, or if the tenant died, then the ground reverted and might be taken up by another. If the tenant of a garden site died, a near relative would have preference in succession to its tenancy.

The produce from an individual holding of land was the property of the individual producer, but all persons in the tribe who wished to do so had the right to take up such area of unappropriated land as could be tilled by them. Likewise the wild fruits, nuts, roots and tubers harvested by anyone were the property of the person who had thus by individual effort conserved and possessed them.

So, likewise, any person might acquire property

in mineral products which he had mined, and in all the objects of his own handicraft. The products of the labor and skill of an individual were his own personal property. These he might hold and use for his own enjoyment, or he might dispose of them by trade for other desired objects, or bestow them by gift; they were his own to do with as he might choose. Thus persons, men or women, who were skillful, industrious, diligent and careful would come into possession of more personal property than the slothful, the unskilled, or the idle, and the owners of property might use it for themselves or give it away in public or private benefactions. But no person, nor any group of persons, nor even a tribe, might monopolize land or water or minerals, or prevent the utilization of the gifts of nature by those who had need of them and who were willing to exert themselves to convert them to use. Such were the commonly accepted ideas among Indians as to property rights.

TRIBAL BOUNDARY LINES

It seems that white people generally do not think of Indian tribes as nations, originally possessing distinct national territories, with definite international boundary lines in most cases. But the fact is that the various tribes were free and independent self-determining nations, each holding dominion over a definite area claimed as its own country and so recog-

nized by neighboring tribes. And each such national territory was delimited by boundary lines,
usually established by treaty-making conventions of
the nations concerned, and marked usually by
natural topographic features, such as streams, hills
and mountains. All such topographic features were
named and well known by the geographers in the
tribes, and by most of the common people. All features marking an intertribal boundary line were
plainly indicated in the treaty stipulations between
the two tribes in interest.

An instance of the determination of boundaries by
Indian tribes is a matter of record in the United
States Court of Claims. This is the claim of the
Omaha tribe, petitioner, against the United States
of America, defendant, No. 31002. In depositions
taken in support of this claim, evidence was given by
Omaha witnesses as to the boundary lines of the
country of the Omahas. The testimony was to the
effect that, starting from the mouth of Nibthaska
(Platte River), at the southeast corner of the Omaha
country, the boundary followed up this stream to the
mouth of a river falling into it from the north,
which the Omahas call Nutanke—that is, "River
Where Nu Abounds." *Nu* is the Omaha name of a
certain species of plant of the bean family which has
large edible tubers. It was an important native food
plant; the tubers were harvested and eaten after
being cooked in the fresh state, or they were dried
and stored for future use. This river which the

Omahas called Nutanke and which they testified was the western boundary line of their country, the boundary between their country and that of the Pawnees, is called on our maps the Loup River. The boundary between the Omahas and the Pawnees followed the course of the Loup River (Nutanke) to the confluence of the North Fork of the Loup, and then along the North Fork to its headwaters. From this point the line ran northward across the watershed to the head of a stream which the Omahas called Hazelnut Creek. It then followed down the course of this stream northward to the point of its confluence with Niubthatha, called Niobrara on our maps. Niobrara is a white man's corruption of the pronunciation of Niubthatha. Hazelnut Creek falls into the Niobrara by a high cascade which the Omahas called Roaring Water. From Roaring Water the line followed the Niobrara to its confluence with Smoky River, the Missouri River of our maps. From the mouth of the Niobrara the line followed down the course of the Missouri to the place of beginning, at the mouth of the Platte. Platte ("Flat") is the French equivalent in meaning of the Omaha name of that river—Nibthaska.

It will be observed that an Omaha in thus describing the boundary lines of his nation began at the southeast and proceeded by the south, west, north and east to the place of beginning. In taking this starting point and following this order, he was but carrying out in this instance, as in all Indian forms and ceremonies, the orientation determined by the apparent motion of the sun around the earth—from sunrise to midday, to evening sunset, and then through the night to sunrise again.

In the description of the Omaha boundary lines as given above, it will be seen that the Platte River was the boundary between the Omahas and their southern neighbors, the Otos. The boundary between the Omahas and their neighbors on the southwest and west, the Pawnees, was formed by the Platte and Loup Rivers, and for a short distance at the northwest by Hazelnut Creek. The boundary at the north, between the Omahas and the Ponkas, was the Niobrara. The Missouri River was the eastern boundary of the Omahas.

Thus it will be seen that streams of water formed all of the boundaries of the Omaha nation without interruption except for the comparatively short distance across the watershed from the head of Loup River to the head of Hazelnut Creek. I asked an old Omaha how the line was marked across the country in such a case, where there was no natural feature to mark it. He replied that boulders were used for line monuments in such cases, and if none were present at the required locations they were transported and placed where they would mark the line. The lines having been established between the Omahas and the Pawnees long ago, before the white people had come to America and brought the horse, there was no means of transport by beasts of burden, and so the monument stones of the border line had to be transported by man power. In order thus to transport the stones, they were placed on a buffalo hide and thus carried by several men in coöperation, holding the hide by its corners.

In the taking of testimony in the case, I was summoned into court as an expert to hear the evidence and to establish the record of certain material facts. In the Brief of Petitioner of this claim, on page 582, is found the following statement:

"The evidence of Gilmore, a disinterested scientific student . . . shows that the Keya-Paha River also bears an Omaha name, the He-azi-ke; also that the Niobrara on the north and the Nebraska or Platte River on the south are Omaha names. The Omahas are shown by the record to have had villages west of the confluence of the Niobrara and the Missouri. . . . Mr. Manypenny drew a straight line . . . to fix the western boundary. But the Omahas instead followed the Loup fork to its headwaters to the northwest. This is established as Indian custom of choosing a natural boundary."

CARRYING THE PIPE

Among many Indian tribes there is practiced a custom which they speak of as "carrying the pipe" to a man. It has been the practice to resort to this ceremony for the accomplishment of various ends, such as to bring about reconciliation after estrangement, to overcome a man's reluctance to perform some duty expected of him, to break down an unreasonable and stubborn opposition, to clear away misunderstandings, to restrain a man from threatened rash and violent actions, to induce or impel a man to fulfill an obligation to which he is averse, or to yield a point in controversy, or for the ending of strife and the making of peace. There are many and diverse occasions for the employment of this means to the end. Ordinarily a man thus approached will not dare, as they say, to "walk over the pipe." He will consider very seriously before refusing the request of one who comes to him "bearing the pipe." The pipe and tobacco have become invested with sacredness from their association in religious ritual as censer and incense, so that their effect is to induce respect, veneration, and awe, and to dispose the mind to serious thought.

I can speak of this custom from actual knowledge of it as practiced in the Arikara tribe, but I understand that other tribes also have the institution. I have had occasion myself to perform this rite. At one time I had an agreement with a man of the Arikara tribe, a priest of one of the sacred bundles, to teach me certain parts of the doctrine of the divine gift of corn, in connection with the ceremonies. I performed my part of the agreement in all particulars, but before the man had performed his part he became vexed, not with me, but with some other persons connected with the affair, and he refused on that account to do as he had agreed. In this difficult situation I "carried the pipe" to him. I provided myself with a regulation red pipestone pipe with ash-wood stem, together with a quantity of the sacred tobacco which is cultivated by the Arikaras, mixed with dried leaves of bearberry and the dried inner bark of red dogwood. I also took along provisions for a dinner, for a feast is always the prescribed conclusion of any formal function among Indians. Taking these materials with me, and accompanied by two other men of the tribe and sustained by their moral support, I went to the priest's house. I let my companions go in first to talk to him and tell him that I desired to speak with him. After they had entered the house and talked with him a while, one of them signaled to me to come in.

So I took the pipe, filled it with the mixture for smoking, and entered the house, carrying the pipe in the prescribed way—that is, with the bowl in my right hand and the stem held horizontal before me with the mouthpiece at the left. I approached him, stooped down, and placed the pipe on the ground before him as he sat, the bowl at his left hand and the mouthpiece at his right. He gravely looked at the pipe and at me as I stood before him, not saying a word for some time. Then he asked me in the way prescribed by custom, "What is this for?" And in the customary manner I replied, giving the reason and purpose of the action. He sat silent for a while, considering the matter.

Then the more elderly of the two men who accompanied me spoke to exhort and persuade and encourage the priest to go on and fulfill his agreement to impart to me the instructions which I was seeking and which he had promised, as he was now reluctant to do. My companion said:

"The Sacred Bundle is the thing which binds the people together. It did so in the ancient time and it does so now. The people have always looked to the keeper of the Sacred Bundle for light and leadership. By its light and under its leadership they walked in the right way. In the ancient days the keepers of the Sacred Bundle were zealous in imparting the teachings to those who earnestly sought them, and the people were faithful to the teaching. Then the people were strong and healthy, of good courage and high spirit. And so should it be with us now. Our people should be united and devoted to the good teachings which we have had from Mother Corn from the ancient days. Mother Corn will keep her promise to us forever, if we do our part.

"Now you must not, on account of any misunderstanding, allow bitter feelings and resentment to abide in your heart and cause you to walk apart from the people. Our people look to you to fulfill your promise and agreement to teach Pahok the mysteries of Mother Corn as he has asked, since he has made the required offerings, according to ancient custom. He has done his part, and he earnestly inquires to know the teachings from Mother Corn. And now you, on your part, must not fail to pass on the teaching which has come down to you in unbroken succession from ancient time. Thus Mother Corn shall be duly honored."

The priest listened attentively to the exhortation until it was finished. Then he yet remained silent, meditatively looking down on the ground, gravely considering the matter. Finally he reached out his hand and took up the pipe. He lighted it, and rose and made the usual smoke offerings to the four quarters, to God above and to Mother Earth. Then he passed the pipe to each of us in turn, that all might be drawn into spiritual accord. When the pipe was smoked out, he emptied and cleaned it in the ritualistic manner, and laid it aside.

Then he spoke of the difficulty which had arisen and how it had offended him. Then he said that now he had put all that away from him; he would not allow that to trouble him any more. So, he said, he was now prepared and willing to fulfill his agreement to instruct me.

I can give another instance of the practical working of this custom in the Arikara tribe. A number of years ago a man whom I knew well had become embittered because of gossip concerning a member of his family. Because of this, the man withdrew himself from meeting with the people in community gatherings and would have no part in any public concerns. Many people were grieved at this state of affairs. Some went and talked with him and begged him not to walk apart from the people. But he felt that he had been too deeply offended, and so he refused to join in community affairs and moodily kept to himself. At last certain ones decided to "carry the pipe" to this man in order to set his heart and mind right again with the people and to bring him again into accord and into participation in tribal and neighborhood affairs. So the pipe was brought and placed before him according to custom, in the manner heretofore described. But his feeling was so bitter that he was unwilling to accept the peace offering. He disregarded it and did not take up the pipe from the ground. He "stepped over the pipe," as the expression is. On his way home from the place where this occurred, he fell in a faint and was found unconscious by someone who was passing that way. This person picked him up, revived him to consciousness, and helped him home. But just as he reached home, he again fell in a swoon. When he recovered consciousness this time and was able to rise and go about, he was frightened and subdued. He expressed the wish to set himself right for the insult he had offered to the pipe in refusing to accept it when brought in good faith. So he resorted to the priest of one of the tribal sacred bundles, confessed his fault, made an offering, and then in penance stood all day before the sacred bundle, fasting and praying for his fault and vowing to be reconciled to the people. After this he recovered his usual health and good spirits, and thereafter again took part in all neighborhood affairs as he had always done before he was wronged.

ESCAPE OF A WAR PARTY

In the northwest part of Nebraska there is a high butte with perpendicular sides like the walls of a great building. Because of the shape of this butte, and because it is composed mostly of a soft rock or hard, firm clay, it is called Court House Rock by the white people. Of course it has other names among the Indian tribes of that region.

This great butte stands out boldly upon the high plain overlooking the Platte River and can be seen for many miles in all directions. The top is almost flat and all sides but one are almost vertical and are bare of vegetation, worn smooth by rain and wind, impossible to climb. But there is a way on one side by which a strong man can climb to the top.

This high lonely butte stands on the borderland between the country of the Pawnees and the country of the Dakotas. The Dakotas and the Pawnees were almost always at war with each other. Many years ago a Pawnee war party was camped near this butte when they were surprised by a war party of Dakotas stronger in number than their own party. In the fight which ensued, the Pawnees were unable to drive their enemies off, but were compelled to take refuge by climbing to the top of the butte. The

Dakotas were unable to follow the Pawnees upon the butte, for the Pawnees were able to guard the single narrow path. But neither could the Pawnees escape again upon the open plain, for the Dakotas securely guarded the descent and could easily kill one after another all who might attempt to come down that way. So it seemed only a question of time before all the Pawnees must die of hunger and thirst upon the top of the rock or come down and give themselves up to death at the hands of their enemies. The camps of the Dakotas surrounded the butte, laying siege to it to starve the Pawnees out.

The Pawnees were in a woeful plight. As the sun rose and traveled across the sky, they could look away for miles and perhaps see flocks of antelopes grazing upon the plain, while their own stomachs were pinched with hunger; and some miles to the south they could see the flashing sunlight gleaming upon the waters of the Platte River, while close at hand, at the foot of the butte, they could see their enemies eating and drinking, which could but serve to aggravate their own hunger and thirst. And at night, when the scorching sun had sunk in the west, they might look away to the eastward, in which direction their homes lay many days' march distant in the beautiful and fruitful valley of the Loup River; and as they looked, the twinkling stars appearing one by one near the eastern horizon must have made them think of the evening camp fires of their home people. And at night the grim chill of the rare air of the high butte gripped their bodies in its clutch. And all the while they must be very vigilant against their enemies to prevent being caught off guard. They all suffered severely, but the captain of the company suffered most of all; for, added to the bodily sufferings which he endured in common with his men, he also suffered extreme mental anguish, for he felt his responsibility on account of his men. Because they had trusted his leadership and had put themselves under his orders, it seemed that now they must all die a horrible death. For himself, he dreaded not death so much as to be the cause of the loss of his brave men. To him this was far more bitter than death. In the nighttime he would go away from the others and cry out in fervent prayer to Tirawa, begging His help, begging that He would show some way to save the men and bring them off safe.

And as the leader prayed, he heard a voice saying, "Look carefully and see if you can find a place where you can climb down from this rock and save your men and yourself." So he prayed earnestly all night, and when daylight came he went along the edges of the butte looking carefully to see if there might be a place where some way might be found by which to go down. At last he found a jutting point of rock near the cliff edge and standing above the level. Below this point the cliff side was smooth and vertical. It occurred to him that this point might be made a means of support from which the men might let themselves down the face of the cliff by a rope. When night came again, after he had posted the sentries to guard the place of ascent from the enemy, he returned to the point of rock and with his knife he cut away the soft weathered rock at its base to make a secure place of fastening for a rope. Then he gathered secretly all the lariats which the company had. These he tied together and then, tying one end securely to the rock which he had prepared, he paid out the rope carefully and found to his joy that it reached the ground below. He made a loop in the rope for his foot, and then he let himself slowly down to the ground; then he climbed back again. When night came again, he posted his sentries so that the enemy might see them at their posts on the side of the butte above the path; but when darkness had fully come, they were all gradually withdrawn. Quietly calling his men about him, he explained his plan and told them how they might all save themselves. He sent his men down the rope, one after another, beginning with the youngest of the company. Last of all, the captain himself came down. He and all his men crept quietly in the darkness through the Dakota lines and escaped safely. The Dakotas directed their vigilance mainly toward the other side of the butte, where lay the only path, and that a very rugged one, between the base and the summit.

The Pawnees never knew how long the Dakotas kept watch about the rock.

FOUR-FOOTED TRIBES

THE FAITHFUL DOG

The dog was the companion and servant of the people over all parts of North America, and previous to the introduction of the horse into the western hemisphere by the Spaniards, the dog was the only domestic animal which the Indians had. After horses were introduced by the Spaniards, they soon came into use by the Indians, and in a comparatively short time they were widely spread over the continent.

But in former days the dog was the only beast of burden that the Indians had. Dogs served as watchers at night, as companions and helpers in the chase, and as bearers of burdens.

Once on a time a hunting party of men of the Dakota nation were in the buffalo grazing country in the time of the winter hunt. Scouts were sent out each day to look for a herd and to bring back report to the officers. One day one of the scouts discovered a herd near a certain lake. He came into camp in the evening, as soon as he could after he found the herd. At once he went, according to the law, and rendered his report to the proper officers. After reporting, he went to his lodge and had his evening meal and then lay down to rest from the weariness of the day's scouting.

The officers held council and made the plans for the next day's activities of the hunting field. Then they sent the herald around the camp to announce the orders for the next day.

At the earliest light next morning, everyone in camp was up and making preparations for the day's work. It was yet early in the day when the hunters reached the lake where the scout had discovered the buffalo herd the previous day. Here they found the buffaloes still feeding. At the command of the officers, the hunters and their dogs were deployed to surround the herd for the slaughter, for the meat supply of the people had become low, and at this opportunity they must replenish their provisions.

The herd was feeding upon a strip of land which was bordered on three sides by a frozen lake. The plan was to advance upon the herd from the base of this strip of land and force them out upon the slippery ice, where the huge animals would be at a disadvantage.

The men and dogs charged upon the herd, and soon the great mass of shaggy beasts was forced out upon the treacherous ice, struggling in great confusion. Many buffaloes were killed before the herd finally reached the shore of the lake and scrambled up the steep bank and fled away over the plain.

The sun was already past the middle of the sky, and the hunters were busy with the work of skinning the carcasses and dressing the beef, making ready to carry back to camp their prize of meat, hides, and other useful products, when suddenly they saw and felt a great change in the sky and in the air. The threatening signs were evident of the swift approach of a blizzard, the dreadful and terrific winter storm of fierce, roaring wind and driving snow and frightful cold which frequently sweeps over the northern plains.

The hunters made haste to reach camp, which had been made in the shelter of the woods not far away. Here a certain number had been detailed by the officers to make camp and to gather firewood, while the others had been taking care of the meat. Now, as the fearful storm threatened, they gathered in the camp, bringing in what they could carry of the meat supply. Soon the hunters were refreshing themselves with freshly broiled steaks, which were much relished by the hungry men, who had eaten nothing since the early morning just before they had broken camp. The dogs too were given their share.

The storm was now upon them in its fury; and all about was a smothering, dizzying swirl of whiteness as impenetrable as the blackness of night. The gale of wind roared unceasingly; the myriad millions of tiny snow particles ground upon each other in the swirl of the storm, each infinitesimal impact adding to the aggregate of reverberation of sound, while the skin tents hummed like enormous drums.

From time to time those who were already in camp shouted, to guide the later comers, who gave answering shouts and came one after another staggering into camp exhausted by the buffeting of the storm. At last only one was missing. The herd scout, who had found and reported the herd the day before,—he and his faithful dog had not yet come in. The fury of the storm throughout the night and the next day prevented the possibility of going to look for the missing man.

Toward the morning following the second night of the storm, its fury abated. As is usual at the end of a blizzard, it was followed by an extraordinary calm. The drifted plain lay as still and white as marble. The stars glistened coldly, like ice crystals in the sky. The air was so clear that the least sound made by any moving creature was magnified in the stillness.

The hunting camp awoke. Suddenly the game call of the great gray wolf was heard. And soon the hunters saw a great number of these gaunt gray creatures out upon the ice of the lake and on the plain, digging out the white mounds which were the snowdrifts about the carcasses of the buffaloes which the hunters had been obliged to leave when the storm came upon them.

And now among the wolf cries another sound was heard—the defiant barking of a dog! It was the scout's dog. The men hurried toward the slaughter field to kill or drive away the wolves. Some wolves were dragging away a buffalo carcass, and from among the snarling, howling pack about this carcass the hunters could distinctly hear the hoarse barking of their missing friend's dog, and occasionally they could hear a strangely muffled shout of a man, sounding as though it came from under the ice.

The hunters finally reached the place to which the carcass had been dragged by the wolves. As the men came near, the wolves ran away and the men saw the dog standing by the carcass for a moment before he fell dead as they reached the place. The men with their knives cut open the abdominal cavity of the carcass and found the missing scout inside, wrapped in his robe in a bed of grass and buffalo hair.

When the storm had come upon him at his work, he had seen that he could not reach the camp, and so he had opened two of the carcasses and removed the internal organs. In one he had made a bed for his dog, and in the other a bed for himself, for protection from the fury of the storm. The dog had kept an opening to his shelter, but his master closed the entrance of his own after he was in, and the hide had frozen solid, making him a prisoner. When the wolves came, the dog was able to free himself and tried to defend his imprisoned master, regardless of his own safety. He had been mortally wounded before the hunters could save him.

As soon as the scout was released, he inquired for the dog, his friend and defender. When he saw that his loyal friend was dead, having given up his life in defense of his master, the scout was deeply moved with grief. He knelt down and stroked the head of the dead dog, and said, "Ah, my friend, you were courageous and faithful unto death. And you died like a brave warrior. You shall have the funeral of a dead warrior."

So with all due ceremony the scout carried the body of the dog to the top of a hill overlooking the lake where he had given up his life in doing his duty. There the scout laid the body. Over it he built up a tomb of boulders which he gathered from the hills. Then he laid upon it offerings of red paint and of food, according to the funeral custom of his people, and they sang the farewell song for the dead.

Ever since that time, this hill has been known to the Dakotas as the Grave of the Dog.

HOW COYOTE CHIEF WAS PUNISHED

Coyote Chief was hunting one day in the Mandan country, and he came upon a buffalo bull grazing. "Brother," he said, "you have nothing to do just now. Let us run a race to see which of us is the swifter."

"All right," said the buffalo, "let us run."

"I shall first go and prepare a place for the race," Coyote Chief said; "then I shall come back for you."

So Coyote Chief found a high, steep bank and placed on the very edge of it a small heap of stones. Then he returned to the buffalo and said: "Everything is now ready. Let us race over to yonder heap of stones which I have set up for a goal. When we are almost to the goal, let us shut our eyes and run as hard as we can." And so they ran toward the heap of stones and the buffalo ran over the bank and was killed by falling, just as Coyote Chief had planned.

But Coyote Chief had nothing with which to skin the buffalo and cut up and prepare the meat. So he walked along a little way and came to a small clump of timber. As he approached the timber he called out, "Brothers, give me a knife," and he was given a knife. Then he went on to another clump of timber. Here he called out, "Brothers, give me an earthen pot," and he was given an earthen pot. He went on again to another clump of timber, where he called out, "Brothers, give me a horn spoon," and he was given a horn spoon.

Then Coyote Chief went back to the place where the buffalo had fallen, and there he built a hunter's lodge of leafy branches of trees. Then he skinned the buffalo and pegged out the skin upon the ground and scraped it. Next he cut up the meat, and some of it he cut into strips and hung up to dry.

Coyote Chief had Fox for a servant, to run errands and to work about the house. And he treated Fox badly and did not give him enough to eat. Fox was hungry, as usual, and tried to help himself to some of the buffalo meat, but Coyote Chief saw him and was angry. He seized a brand from the fire and thrust it into Fox's face, burning him thereby. Fox was hurt so badly that he decided to run away, but he wished first to be revenged upon Coyote Chief. So he went around to all the other animals and told them how badly he had been used by Coyote Chief. The animals were sorry for him and seemed willing to help him to punish Coyote Chief. So they held a meeting and talked over the matter to decide upon the best way to do this. The decision of the council was that they should all go over to his house that night and eat up all his meat while he was asleep.

Coyote Chief had worked hard all day to take care of his meat and had not taken time to eat much. Being tired after his day's work, he went to bed early. But he was anxious lest someone might come and take his meat while he slept; so, before going to sleep, he said: "Now, my members, you must watch for me while I sleep. My eyes, if anyone peeps in, you must stare hard at him. My ears, if you hear a sound, you must wriggle. My arms, if anyone comes in, you must thrash around. My legs, if anyone comes near, you must kick." Then he went to sleep.

That night all the animals gathered at Coyote Chief's house, but they were afraid to touch anything till they were sure he was sound asleep. So they sent Magpie first to peep at the door. Magpie went and peeped in and saw Coyote Chief's eyes staring hard at him, and he went back and said, "He is not asleep, for his eyes stared at me."

After a time, Crow was sent to find if Coyote Chief was not asleep. Crow flew up and perched by the smoke hole. When he looked in, Coyote Chief's ears began to wriggle. Crow went back and told the animals that Coyote Chief could not be asleep, for as soon as he looked in, Coyote Chief's ears began to wriggle.

A little later, Jack Rabbit was sent to look. Jack Rabbit pushed in a little at the door, and Coyote Chief's arms began to move up and down. So Jack Rabbit went back and reported that Coyote Chief must still be awake.

The animals again waited, and then sent Fox. Fox went inside, and then Coyote Chief's legs began to kick, so Fox ran out and told the others that Coyote Chief was still awake.

Now, after waiting quite a long time, the animals sent Mouse. Mouse went in and saw that Coyote Chief seemed to be sound asleep. He went up and ran over his legs and there was no motion; then he ran over his chest, and still Coyote Chief was not disturbed. At last he ran over his face, and Coyote Chief did not stir. So Mouse went and told the others that Coyote Chief was surely asleep. Then they came in and ate up all the meat except a few scraps which dropped while they were eating. When they had finished eating, they went away without having wakened Coyote Chief.

The next morning when Coyote Chief awoke, he was very hungry, because he had eaten little the day before and had worked hard; but he found that his meat was all gone, and he said to himself, "Oh, why did I not eat the meat yesterday instead of waiting!" Then, because he was so hungry, he searched about on the ground and found some scraps of meat and some small bits of fat. All these he gathered upon a robe. He put fresh wood upon the fire, and then sat down by the fireplace with the robe over his knees to eat the little he had. But just then a spark shot out from the fire and lighted on his hand, which hurt him so that he jumped up suddenly, spilling into the fire all the shreds of meat and fat which he had so carefully gathered.

So Coyote Chief got none of his meat and was punished for the bad way he had treated Fox.

THE COYOTE'S BOX-ELDER KNIFE

This is a story which was told among the people of the Arikara tribe to young boys of ten or twelve years of age to stir their imagination. The story relates that a man was sitting in his eagle pit on a distant and lonely hill, intent on catching eagles to obtain their plumes to be used in making war bonnets and badges of military honors.

It should be said that men who went out to capture eagles made pits on high and remote places frequented by eagles. These pits were so made that a man could sit in one while he waited and watched for the eagles to come. The pits had poles laid across them, and on these poles a covering of sod was laid so as to conceal the pit and all evidence of its presence. A dead rabbit or some other bait was fastened on the surface of the pit cover in such position that when the eagle alighted to take it in his talons the man could reach his hand through an opening and seize the eagle by the feet.

So this story tells of a man who was sitting thus in his eagle pit. While he was waiting, he heard a voice in the distance crying out and saying in words like the speech of a human being,

"I want a knife! I wish to have a knife!"

The man cautiously peeped out from his hiding place to see who might be the speaker. To his surprise, the man could see no human being anywhere, but down at the foot of the hill he saw a coyote trotting along in the coulee. It was the coyote which was crying for a knife. And now as the man listened he heard another voice answering the coyote's cry and saying,

"Come here!"

Then the man saw the coyote go to the place from which came the voice. At that place there stood a box-elder tree. It was the box-elder tree which had called in answer to the cry of the coyote. When the coyote reached the place where the box-elder tree was, the tree said:

"Do you now take one of these my seeds in its husk, which, as you see, resembles the shape of a knife. If you will take up one of them and strike it upon the ground, it will become for you veritably a knife. So you shall have what you require."

The coyote did as he was told by the tree, and the seed became a knife, which he carried along with him as he went on his way.

Presently the coyote saw a fat badger ambling up the next hill. The coyote pursued the badger and soon overtook it. Now the coyote with his knife cut the badger's throat, so that it soon bled to death. Then the coyote looked for his knife again, but there was no knife anywhere to be seen. He found only the box-elder seed again, as it was at the first.

THE BEAN MOUSE

Indians generally have respect for all forms and manifestations of life, for all the species of plants and animals. Especially they highly regard those species of living creatures, either plant or animal, which appear to have most worthy qualities. To all such they give marked respect, and they like to associate these creatures in a symbolic way with their ceremonies and acts of formal worship. Before they

knew Christianity, they liked to include relics of
certain species in their shrines so that they might
piously meditate upon them, thus gaining help to
direct their minds in worship. And since they have
become Christians, they like to bring such relics into
the sanctuaries of their churches. Thus they will
bring in at their proper seasons parts of certain
plants as reminders of the good gifts of the plants
and as tokens of their due thanks for those gifts. In
autumn they will bring in for contemplation any
ground beans which they may have found along the
paths of the bean mouse where the little animal has
dropped them while carrying them to its storage
chamber. Such relics serve to aid men in holding
thoughts of gratitude both to the plant which gave
its gift of food, and to the intelligent and industrious little animals whose labors have garnered the
gift.

The bean mouse and its works are regarded with
admiration and reverence by the people of the
various Indian tribes which benefit by its labor. In
the fall, after the bean mice have harvested their
beans and laid them up in their storehouses for the
winter, the people often go out alone and sit upon
the lap of Mother Earth near some such storehouse
in some quiet place under the open sky, reverently
and thankfully meditating upon the mysteries of
Nature and the bounties of Providence in Nature.

An old man of the Teton Dakotas, who lived
upon the Standing Rock Reservation on the upper

Missouri River, went out to the vicinity of a bean mouse's storehouse to meditate and pray. Thinking himself to be alone in the presence of the powers of Nature, the old man gave expression to his religious feeling in a prayerful meditation which was overheard and recorded by another man who was within hearing, but unobserved by the old man. The words of his meditation may be translated as follows:

Thou who art holy, pity me and help me, I pray. Thou art small, but thou art sufficiently large for thy place in the world. And, though weak, thou art sufficiently strong for thy work, for Holy Wakantanka constantly strengthens thee. Thou art also wise, for the wisdom of holiness is with thee constantly.

May I be wise in my heart continually, for if holy wisdom leads me on, then this shadow-troubled life shall come into constant light.

GRATITUDE TO THE BEAN MOUSE

Among all tribes is found a strong popular feeling of affection and respect for the bean mouse. The Omahas have a saying that "the bean mice are very industrious people; they even help human beings."

All persons of the Dakota (or Sioux) nation who have talked with me about the bean mice have always said that they never took away any beans from the mice without making some payment in kind, for it would be wicked and unjust to steal the beans from the mouse people without making any return. They therefore put back some corn, some suet, or some other food, in exchange for the beans they took. They said that thus both they and the bean-mouse people had the advantage of a variety in their food supply. The Dakotas have a popular story which exemplifies their attitude toward the bean mouse:

"A certain woman plundered the storehouse of some Hintunka people [bean mice]. She robbed them of their entire food supply without giving anything in return. The next night this woman heard a woman in the woods crying and saying,

" 'O, what will my poor children do now?'

"It was the voice of the Hintunka woman crying over her hungry children.

"The same night the unjust woman who had done the wrong had a dream. In her dream, Hunka, the spirit of kinship of all life, appeared to her and said:

" 'You should not have taken the food from the Hintunka people. Take back the food to them, or some other in its place, or else your own children shall cry from hunger.'

"Next morning the woman told her husband of this vision, and he said,

" 'You would better do as Hunka tells you to do.'

"But the woman was hard-hearted and perverse, and would not make restitution for the wrong she had done.

"A short time afterward a great prairie fire came, driven by a strong wind, and swept over the place where the unjust woman and her family were camping. The fire consumed her tipi and everything it contained, and the people barely escaped with their lives. They had no food nor shelter; they wandered destitute on the prairie, and the children cried from hunger."

THE LOST BOY AND THE BEAN MOUSE

One of the folk stories of the Omahas having for their purpose the inculcation of discipline and self-control in children is connected with the ground bean and the bean mouse. It is a story which has points of likeness to the Roman story of Romulus and Remus; but in the Omaha story it was not a she-wolf, but a gentle, compassionate bean-mouse mother which was the foster mother.

The story concerns the adventures of twin brothers. In their helpless infancy their father, a famous hunter, returned to his house one day to find that in his absence a monster had killed his wife and that one of the twins was gone. The monster, after killing the mother, had carried away one of the babies and cast it in the woods, but the other he had left in the house, where the father found and cared for it when he returned. The one of the twins which was exposed in the woods was found and cared for by a kind old bean-mouse mother, who fed it on the best she had, which was ground beans from her food stores. So the twin brothers were reared separately until they were large enough to run about and play. The father, each day when he left the house, provided food for the boy during his own absence and cautioned him against dangers and gave him directions as to his actions.

After his father was gone, he heard a voice singing :

> Younger brother, thou hast a father,
> And so drink soup.
> But I have no father,
> And so I eat ground beans.

Then he went to the door and looked out and saw a little boy like himself. He called to the other little boy to come and play with him, but it was long before he could overcome the shyness and timidity of his visitor. These visits continued day after day until finally the wild brother was captured and recognized by the father as his lost son. Thereafter the twins were reunited and reared under the care and instruction of the father, and the two brothers had many strange adventures together, overcoming all their difficulties and dangers by courage and determination. The purpose of the story is to teach boys to be strong-hearted, and to train their own powers of observation and of endurance, and also to teach the interrelation and interdependence of human beings and all the more lowly forms of life, both animals and plants, and to inculcate a proper regard and respect therefor.

THE BLACK-TAILED DEER THAT TALKED

North Dakota has a number of places to which interesting legends and myths are attached. One such place is a butte not far from Schmitt, on the south side of the Missouri River, on the road between Mandan and Cannon Ball. It is west of Eagle Beak Butte.

The story of this butte is a Mandan myth. A long time ago the Mandans lived in a village which was on a level place just north of the Bad Water Creek, which white people call Little Heart River. At the west of this place there is a range of high hills. The Mandans lived at the Bad Water village in a time long before white men had come across the great water, and so there were no horses in the country. The people had no animals except dogs to help them carry their burdens. And of course they had never heard of the thunder-irons (guns) which strike and kill the deer and other game at long distance. So it was hard work to obtain their supply of meat and to carry it home to their houses.

A man who lived in the Bad Water village had dug a deer pit in a place among the hills west of the village and had cunningly covered it over to make it appear not different from the ground about it. By this means he hoped to capture a deer, whose flesh would be food for his family, whose skin would be useful for clothing, whose sinews would be used for thread, and whose bones would be used for making awls and needles and other useful implements and tools. Its horns would be used to make garden rakes for working the ground of his family's garden.

One night in autumn there was a snowfall, the first of the season. The man went out early the next morning into the hills to look at his trap to see if it might have caught something during the night. As he approached the place, he saw that the cover was broken through; and when he came near and looked in, he was rejoiced to see that he had captured a fine large black-tailed deer.

Now when he came to the edge of the pit and looked down at his prize, the deer looked up at him and spoke to him, saying, "O, man, do not kill me, but let me go free from the pit. If you release me, you will do well." The man was startled to hear the deer speak to him, and he was disappointed to think of losing his prize. But he thought to himself, "This is something mysterious; I must give heed; I must not defy the Mysterious Power, but must listen to the message; for it must be that the Mysterious Power wishes to impart something to me through this animal as its messenger." So, as he thus hesitated in doubt, the deer again appealed to him, requesting to be set free. But the man spoke of his duty to his family, who looked to him for food and for clothing. Again the deer spoke and said, "Indeed you do well to think of your family, and your endeavor to provide for them as well as you can is prompted by both your love and your duty. But I say to you that you will do well if you allow me to go. If you do so, I promise that you will have success in hunting; you shall find game abundant for the needs of yourself and your family. And when war comes upon your people, you shall be victorious over the enemy. So shall you be remembered among your people for bravery."

The man gave heed to what the deer said to him, and he dared not disobey the message which had come to him in this mysterious way. So now he began to dig down the side of the pit so that the deer could come out. When he had finished he said to the deer, "Now you may go." Then the deer came up the incline from the pit and ran down across the Bad Water Creek away toward the Eagle Beak Hill. As he ran, the new-fallen snow flew behind him from his hoofs in a white cloud, and he sang a song:

> I was glad when I saw the first snow,
> But I almost lost the sight of day.

The man watched the deer as it ran, and when it approached a conical butte west of Eagle Beak Butte he observed that the butte opened with a loud roaring sound and the deer entered and he saw it no more, and then the butte closed again as before.

The man went home pondering these things in his mind. As time passed, events came true as they had been promised to him in the message spoken by the deer. He became renowned among his people for his skill and success in the chase, for his generosity to the old people and to the sick and poor, and he attained many honors for his deeds of valor in warfare against the enemies of his people.

Ever since that time the Mandans have called the butte into which the deer disappeared, after its release from the pit, The Lodge of the Black-tailed Deer.

THE WAR EAGLE AND THE JACK RABBIT

One time a party of Mandan men went into a lonely place among the hills far away from the village, to enter their eagle pits for the purpose of catching eagles to obtain their plumes. One of the men had made his pit far out, at some distance from any of the others. Another day, as he was coming away from his eagle pit, returning to the village, he stopped and sat down upon the top of a high hill from which he could enjoy a grand view of the landscape. Thus he sat looking about over the quiet hills and valleys, beyond the bright gleam which showed the course of the river winding in and out among the green trees along its borders, far away to the dim sky line. Far away on one side he saw a number of elks feeding, and on the other side he saw a band of graceful antelopes. A doe and her fawn were browsing upon some bushes down near the river. Aloft he saw the white clouds sailing in the bright blue sky; below he saw their shadows moving over the earth, now up a hillside and over its crest, and then swiftly across a little valley and up the next hillside. While he sat enjoying the beauty of the scene, he observed a war eagle chasing a jack rabbit. The jack rabbit continually dodged and circled, trying to escape as the eagle swooped toward him. The eagle had swooped several times and just missed striking the rabbit.

Gradually the chase came near to the place where the man was seated. The eagle was closely pursuing the rabbit and made a tremendous swoop towards him. But the rabbit escaped by leaping into the man's robe as he sat with it loosely draped about his shoulders and knees.

Then the eagle said, "Put that rabbit away from you! He is my prey. I intend to eat him."

But now the rabbit appealed to the man and said, "I have thrown myself upon your kindness. Do not turn me away, I beg of you. If you save me, you shall hereafter have success in your undertakings and you shall become a great man."

Then the eagle spoke again, saying, "His words are not true. Turn him away. He can do nothing for you. I, myself, will make you great if you will do as I request. It is I who speak the truth. My feet are not held to the earth; I can fly in the air far above the earth. I am successful in all the things I attempt."

Once more the jack rabbit made his plea: "Believe him not, and do not turn me away! Even though I must remain upon the ground and cannot fly like the eagle, still I have knowledge proper to my conditions of life, and I know how to do many things suitably and successfully."

The man made his decision in favor of the jack rabbit and saved him from the eagle. The jack rabbit kept his promise to the man, for he gave him of his own powers and made him successful in his undertakings and helped him with good and wise counsel in times of trouble and doubt and perplexity. So the man gained great renown and honor and influence among his people.

THE SONG OF THE OLD WOLF

There is a story told among the people of the Dakota nation that once on a time an old man went out to be alone upon a high hill above the Missouri River to give himself to meditation and prayer. He chose this situation because of the grandeur and majesty of the' view of the great sweep of the prairie plains and hills, one hill beyond another, away and away to the far horizon. Below flowed the wonderful and mysterious river, whose waters came down from the mighty mountains at the west and rolled on and on past the villages of many different nations, finally reaching the Great Salt Water.

As the old man thus sat meditating and considering all the manifestations of life and power and mystery of earth and sky, he espied out upon the prairie a group of wolves trotting toward the river. When they reached the river, they plunged in and swam across to the other side, all but one old one who was now too enfeebled by age to dare try his strength against the swift and powerful current of the river.

This old wolf sat down upon the bank of the river and watched his companions as they swam across and trotted away out of sight on the other side. When they had disappeared from sight, he raised his muzzle toward the sky and mournfully sang in a man's voice the following song: [1]

> All o'er the earth I've roamed,
> I've journeyed far and wide;
> My spirit haste and go,
> I'm nothing, nothing now,
> I'm nothing, nothing now.

> Missouri River, flow,
> Thou sacred water flow;
> My spirit haste and go,
> I'm nothing, nothing now,
> I'm nothing, nothing now.

[1] The translation of "The Song of the Old Wolf" is by Dr. A. McG. Beede, of Fort Yates, North Dakota. The original song in the Dakota language is as follows:

Maka takomni	Mni-shoshe yayo,
Tehan omawani;	Mni-wakan yayo.
Mi nagi ya yayo,	Mi nagi ya yayo.
Wana ma takuni.	Wana ma takuni!
	Wana ma takuni!
	Ooooooooh!

After the old wolf had sung this song, he wearily made his way to the top of a hill and lay down in the warm sunshine, in the shelter of a rock, and there waited until his spirit went away.

And so now, when old men of the Dakota nation find the infirmities of age creeping upon them, and feel as though they had been left behind in life's march, they will often go out alone to the summit of some high hill overlooking the Missouri River and, sitting there in solitude, will muse upon their activities and noteworthy deeds in the past, of their companions of former days now long gone from them, and contrast all this with their present inactivity and loneliness. Then they will sadly and quaveringly sing this "Song of the Old Wolf."

TRIBES OF THE AIR

WHY GEESE MIGRATE

The Teton Dakotas have a story which says that "long, long time ago" (lila ehañna) the goose nation did not migrate to the south in the autumn, but remained here throughout the wintertime. Because of the rigor of the winter, most of the people of the goose nation perished, so that they were always a small and weak nation. At last one goose had a dream of the southland, that it was pleasant even in winter, that the winter there was mild, and that there was plenty of food there. So she began teaching the other geese that they should practice flying more and thus make their wings strong so that the geese could fly to the southland before wintertime. Some people of the goose nation believed the vision and began to practice flying to make their wings strong for the autumn journey. This caused discussion and dissension in the nation, and a law was made which banished the goose which had the vision. So they drove her out from among them. She practiced flying all summer and made her wings strong, so that in the autumn she was able to fly to the pleasant southland of which she had dreamed. The Mysterious Power which had given her the vision guided her on the long journey, and she lived pleasantly through the wintertime. After the first thunder in the springtime, she flew back north to her nation. As always before, many of them had died during the cold wintertime from the fury of the storms and the scarcity of food. But she told them how pleasantly she had passed the time in the southland, and they saw in what good health she was, and many more of them now believed her vision and her teaching. It was in this way that the geese learned to fly away to the southland in the autumn to escape the storms and cold of winter in this land.

HOW THE MEADOW LARK
WON THE RACE

A young man named Piya had a beautiful and lovely young wife, and she was carried away by an evil monster who kept her hidden in his dwelling,

The young man's grandmother was a very wise old woman. She had great knowledge of the birds and beasts, and of the trees and other plants, and she had mysterious powers and could do many wonderful things. She had taught her grandson many things also, so that he too had uncommon knowledge and powers.

Now when the monster stole his wife away, he came to his grandmother to ask her to help him recover his wife. Before he came to her, his grandmother knew he was in trouble, so when he came he found her waiting for him. She said, "I will prepare you for this quest; but first bring to me a wolf, a turtle and a meadow lark." Then she brought him food; and after he had eaten and rested, he set out to find the wolf, the turtle and the meadow lark. As he journeyed, he found all of them, one after another, and invited them to eat with him. Then he told of his grandmother's wish to have them to aid him in his quest. Each of them consented to help provided the old woman would give him the thing most desired. The wolf said he wished to have a better fur coat, so that the cold breath of old Waziya, the Old Man Winter, would not chill him. The turtle said, "Insects bite me; I will help you if I shall be given protection from insects which suck my blood." The meadow lark said, "My voice is harsh, and I can sing but one note, and the magpie laughs at me. I will help you if I may be given a pleasing voice so that I can make the magpie ashamed." So the young man, Piya, the wizard, together with his three friends, the wolf, the turtle and the meadow lark, came back to the tipi of his grandmother.

She was waiting and expecting him, and said, "Grandson, I knew you would come and bring with you those whom I want." She invited them into her tipi and prepared food and set it before them. The next morning Piya told his grandmother that these friends he had brought had promised to help him if each should be given what he most desired. Then she told them that if they would help her grandson, she would give each one what he most wished. So they were all agreed. She told the wolf she wished him to give her grandson the cunning by which he could follow a hidden trail and find hidden things; she asked the turtle to give him the sense by which he could locate water, so that he should be able to avoid perishing of thirst in a desert land; and the lark was to give him power to hide himself in the open prairie. In return for these gifts the wolf was to have for himself and all his people warm fur clothing, so that they could laugh at Waziya when he would blow his cold breath upon them. The turtle was promised that he should have the hard, tough covering which he asked, so that insects could not bite him. The meadow lark was given a pleasing voice, so that his songs would make the magpie ashamed.

After the agreement was made, the old woman

told them that the quest on which they had to go would take them into a country where there would be no trees nor much grass nor open trail, and but little water in the hidden springs.

So the wizard, Piya, and his companions, the wolf, the turtle and the meadow lark, set out upon the quest after the old woman had instructed them. The wolf taught him how to find hidden trails; the meadow lark taught him how to be hidden without covering, and the turtle taught him how to find hidden water springs.

So the help of these friends, together with the powers he already possessed, enabled Piya finally to discover where his wife was hidden by the monster, and to rescue her.

So they all came back to the tipi of the old woman. They all rejoiced—the young woman because she had been rescued from the power of the monster; the young man, Piya, because he had found his wife; and the wolf, the turtle and the meadow lark because they were to have the gifts which they had most desired. The old woman prepared a feast, and they feasted until far into the night.

Next morning the old woman gave to the wolf, the turtle and the meadow lark each the gift for which he had asked as a reward for helping the young man, and they set out together on the trail to return to their homes. As they journeyed they talked about the gifts which they had received. They fell into argument, each claiming that his gift was the best, and soon they were quarreling and were about to fight. But just then a young man came along the trail, and he asked them why they were quarreling. They told him. He said that quarreling was foolish and would decide nothing, but that the only way to determine whose gift was the best was to find out which would help most in a trial of skill. The wolf proposed a trial in hunting, but the meadow lark and the turtle said they could not hunt. The turtle proposed a swimming contest, but the wolf and the meadow lark said they could not swim. Then the meadow lark in his turn proposed a contest in singing, for he was very proud of his gift, but the wolf and the turtle protested that they could not sing.

The young man suggested that they run a race. To this they all agreed. The young man told them they must run past a plum thicket, across a marsh and up to the top of a certain hill. There they would find white clay and colored clay. The winner of the race would be the one that first brought back to him some of the white clay. They set out upon the race. The wolf and the turtle were running side by side; but the meadow lark fell far behind.

When the wolf came near the plum thicket, he saw a bundle laid up in the forks of a plum bush. He paused and sniffed toward it, and the scent of it was strange to him, and he became curious about it, and wanted to find out what was in the bundle.

He asked the turtle to wait. The turtle said he would wait for him at the marsh. The wolf walked all around the bush and looked carefully at the bundle. Then he rose up against the bush and sniffed at the bundle, but still he could not make out what was in it. He could not quite reach the bundle, so he leaped to try to pull it down. But as he did so, the thorns pricked him. He jumped again and missed the bundle, but was pricked again by the thorns. Now he became angry and determined he would get the bundle. After jumping many times and being always pricked by the thorns, so that he had many wounds on his sides and back, he finally pulled down the bundle. He was so angry that in his vexation he energetically shook it about, so that it was shaken open and its contents smeared his wounds. This made his wounds itch so severely that he had to scratch himself, but this made him itch the more. He was in such torment that he scratched madly and tore his fur coat and was bleeding, and so he forgot the race.

The turtle ran on to the marsh and waited there as he had promised. After he had waited a long time, he concluded that the wolf had deceived him and had gone on to the hill. Then he saw a small white puffball. It looked like a lump of white clay, and the thought came to him that he could deceive the young man with it and get even with the wolf for the trick that he supposed the wolf had played upon him. So he took the puffball back and showed it to the young man. Neither the meadow lark nor the wolf had yet returned, and so the young man told the turtle that he was the first to return bringing something to show that he had been to the top of the hill.

Now when the meadow lark ran by the plum thicket, he saw the wolf jumping about one of the bushes trying to reach something which was there; so the meadow lark was encouraged to think that he might still have some chance in the race. He ran on to the marsh, and there he saw the turtle waiting; so he was still more encouraged. He then ran on all the way to the top of the hill. He was so anxious and flustered when he reached there that, instead of the white clay which the young man had specified as the token of having been to the goal, he made a mistake and picked up a lump of the yellow clay and turned to carry it back to the young man. As he was crossing over the marsh again, he stumbled and dropped the lump of clay into the black mud. He picked it up and hurried on, not stopping to clean off the black mud. When he came near to the young man, he saw the turtle sitting there and smiling and looking very satisfied. The meadow lark then thought he had lost the race. He was so disappointed and discouraged that he wept. His tears washed the black mud off from the lump of clay and made a black stripe, while the yellow clay itself was washed down over the whole front of his clothes.

At last the wolf came back, scratching and howling in his misery. Great patches of fur were torn from his clothes, and his skin was raw and sore. The turtle taunted the wolf for his crying. He swaggered about and boasted that nothing could make him whimper and cry. The young man said that the turtle was the first to return, but that he must make good his boast that nothing could make him whimper if he should lose. The turtle declared that he would prove all he said in any way the young man should require. The young man then placed the puffball upon the turtle's back. The puffball very quickly increased in size and weight so that it was all the turtle could bear. It continued to increase in size until the turtle was borne down by it to the ground and his legs were bent. Still the puffball continued to grow until the turtle's body was pressed flat by it, and his breath was pressed out of his body, and he lay as if he were dead. Then the puffball became as light as a feather and turned black. The turtle recovered his breath a little, but he was unable to straighten his legs or to regain the form of his body; so he was ashamed and drew in his head under his thick skin.

Then the young man laughed loud and long at the plight of the wolf, the turtle and the meadow lark, and told them now who he really was. He told them that he was Iktomi, the Trickster. He told them that because they had foolishly quarreled about the good gifts which the old woman had given to them, instead of making good use of them, they had given him the opportunity to play this trick upon them, the marks of which would be upon them and upon their people forever. He said that because the wolf had meddled with something which was none of his affair, he had brought upon himself the torments of the mange, and so it would always be with his people whenever they should do as he had done. He said that because the turtle had attempted to win by cheating, his legs and the legs of all his people should always be short and bent and their bodies should be flattened, so they could never run in a race. And because he had lied in saying the puffball was white clay, therefore he and his people should never again be able to speak, and they should always hide their heads for shame. As for the meadow lark, the young man said he had won the race, but because he had brought back the yellow clay instead of the white, therefore his clothes and the clothes of his people should always be yellow in front and there should be a black stripe over the yellow.

CHILDREN AND THE MEADOW LARK

One summer day a group of Teton Dakota children, the older ones ten or eleven years of age, and others younger, were playing on the prairie not far from the village. On this occasion, as was usual and quite natural, the common things of their familiar surroundings furnished subjects for their talk and play. The native grasses and wild flowers of the prairie and the birds, insects and other animals held perpetual charm and delight for the children. The familiarity of all these things in their ordinary surroundings only added to their interest by friendly association.

Their prime favorite among all the birds was the cheery meadow lark. Many pretty stories and pleasant associations are connected with this bird, which the people of the Dakota nation like to call "the bird of promise."

One little girl of the group was talking to the other children, her companions, about the meadow lark. As is quite common with Indians, even children, she made some drawings to illustrate her talk. On a wide bare place in the trail which wound its way across the prairie, she had drawn these pictures in the dust. In a circle about four feet in diameter she had drawn a representation of a camp circle of tipis. Among the tipis she had drawn the figures of dogs, as they would be seen usually in an Indian camp. Outside the circle she had drawn the figures of ponies, just as ordinarily they would be found grazing outside the camp circle.

Farther away she had drawn some figures of buffaloes. And some distance away up the trail on the other side, she had drawn a meadow lark on the wing as if it were up in the sky. A faint circle was drawn about the figure of the bird. From the center of the circle of tipis a zigzag line was drawn to the meadow lark in the sky.

The little girl was teaching her companions concerning the relationship of living things in this world. She said: "The bird of promise is our friend. It likes to be around our dwellings, and likes to see our people happy. While it has been flying about over the prairie and about the camps of our people, it has been observing us and all living things on the earth. At daydawn it flies circling upward into the sky, when the light of the rising sun lights up the earth and sparkles on the dewdrops on the grass and the flowers. So it goes up and tells Wakantanka what is needed by our people, and by the animals and the trees and the flowers and all living things. And it comes back singing songs to tell each one of all these living beings what Wakantanka is going to do for that one on that day, whether tree or flower or human being, and even all living beings. If I have been well-behaving, I am glad and eager to hear what the bird of promise will sing to me when he comes back. But if I have been ill-behaving, I am afraid to hear what he will sing to me."

THE HORNED LARK

The name of the horned lark in the Dakota language is *ishtaniche-tanka* ("big eye-tufts"), from the tuft of feathers which it has over each eye. It is for the same reason that we call it "horned."

The Dakotas say that this little bird foretells the weather. They say that when a hot dry time is coming in the summer, the bird sounds a single sharp little note; but when rain is coming, the bird is glad and continuously sings loudly and joyously, *magazhu, magazhu, magazhu!* In the Dakota language the word for rain is *magazhu*. Thus the bird is singing its joy for the rain which is coming.

The name of this bird is *hupa-hishe* in the Hidatsa language. In that language the word for moccasin is *hupa*; the word *hishe* means wrinkled. This bird is called "wrinkled moccasin" because of its appearance in its characteristic habit of crouching upon the ground, where, by its grayish-brown color and its black markings, it is made inconspicuous and hardly distinguishable, suggesting the appearance of a ragged, useless old moccasin.

The Hidatsas have a story that this bird was once acting as a spy in enemy country. While it sat in its characteristic attitude of inconspicuousness, two of the enemy were coming along, and one thought he saw something. He stopped and said to his companion,

"Wait, what is that over there?"

His companion glanced over and saw what appeared to him like nothing but a ragged, rotten old fragment of a worn-out moccasin, and answered,

"O, that is just an old wrinkled moccasin."

So the bird escaped his enemies, and it is from this that the people call him *hupa-hishe*.

THE CHICKADEE

The chickadee is a very popular bird among all the Indian tribes where it is known. They all have many stories and sayings about it. They say of it that, though small, it is a very wise bird. It is like the wise men, the doctors and teachers among the people, who are learned in mysteries and the wonderful things of nature, who keep a calendar of the cycle of the days, months and seasons through the year by cutting marks upon a piece of wood which they have prepared for that purpose.

This wise little bird is said also to keep account of the months. It is said that "in the beginning" the task of keeping account of the months was assigned to the chickadee. But instead of making notches in a piece of wood as the wise men do, this wise bird's method is to make notches in its tongue; thus in September its tongue is single-pointed, in October it has two points, in November three, and so on until February, when it is said that its tongue has six points. Then in March its tongue is again single-pointed and the count is begun again. So, it is said, the chickadee has been keeping count of the months since the long ago, in the dim past, when the task was assigned to it in the time of beginnings, in the time when the evil powers and monsters struggled mightily to overcome the good, and to destroy mankind by sending fierce storms and heavy snowfalls and shuddering cold winds upon the face of the earth. It was thus that the evil powers sought to discourage and to overcome mankind.

And so it is said that at one time the evil powers supposed that by stress of a long siege of cold and storms they had reduced mankind to famine. At this time they chose to send the chickadee as a messenger to find out the conditions and to bring back word to them.

Now when the chickadee came on his mission and appeared at the dwellings of men, he was invited to enter. He was courteously given a place by the fireside to rest and warm himself. Then food was brought to him. After he had eaten and refreshed himself, he was anointed with fat, which was a symbol of plenty; then he was painted with red paint, which was for a symbol of the power and mystery of life. After these ceremonies and marks of respect, his hosts quietly composed themselves to give attention to whatever their visitor should have to say as to the purpose of his visit. When he had stated his mission, his hosts held counsel and formulated a reply for the messenger to take back to those who had sent him. He was bidden to say to them that mankind was still living and hopeful, and they ever would be; that they could not be daunted by discouragement, nor defeated by storms and stress, nor vanquished by hunger, nor overcome by any hardships; and that there never would be a time when there should not be men upon the earth. So this is the message which the chickadee brought to the evil powers which had sought to overcome mankind.

THE SONG OF THE WREN

The incident of this story occurred in the long ago in the country of the Pawnee nation, in the broad expanse of the Platte River country in what is now the state of Nebraska. The event was in the distant past before the Pawnees had ever seen a white man, or any of his works or strange devices. The people of the Pawnee nation lived in villages of houses built in the manner in which the houses of Pawnees had been built for generations. Near their villages lay their fields of corn and other crops which they cultivated to supply themselves with food.

It was a beautiful morning in early summer. The sky was clear and bright; the dawn-light was showing in the eastern sky. All the landscape lay as though still sleeping. There was no movement anywhere. A thoughtful priest had risen and had walked out upon the prairie away from the village so that he might view and meditate upon the beauty and mystery of the firmament of the heavens and of the plane of earth, and of the living creatures thereon, both animal creatures and plant creatures, for in his mind both were equally wonderful and equally interesting, as showing the power and the wisdom of the Great Mystery. And so he walked, pondering upon all the beauty and mystery which lay about him, while the face of Mother Earth was still

moist with the dew of sleep. In a moment the first
rays of the sun shone across the land, touching into
sparkling brilliance the myriads of dewdrops, while
a gentle movement ran through all the grasses and
the wild flowers as they swayed to the rippling
of the gentle morning breeze which pulsed over the
prairie at the first touch of the morning gleam.

Where a moment before all had been so still and
so silent, now there was movement and sound. Birds
of many kinds raised their tuneful voices, showing
their joy in life and in the beauty of the morning.
The priest, whose mind and heart were open to all
this beauty and melody, stood still and listened. In
a moment, among all the bird-songs he heard one
which was clearer and more remarkable than any of
the others. This song was a most joyous, cheerful
sound, like happy laughter. As he approached, he
found that the joyous, laughing song came from a
very tiny brown bird, no larger than his thumb. It
was a wren, so small, so insignificant in comparison
to the size and brilliant plumage of many of the
other birds, yet it appeared to be the most whole-
hearted in joy and praise and delight in life, as the
sweet stream of music welled from its little throat.

The priest looked at the tiny bird, and wisely considered. He said to himself: "The Great Mystery
has shown me here a wise teaching for my people.
This bird is small and weak, but it has its proper
place in the world of life, and it rejoices and gives
thanks with gladness. Everyone can be happy, for

happiness is not from without, but from within, in properly fitting and fulfilling each his own place. The humblest can have a song of thanks in his own heart."

So he made a song to be sung in a great religious ritual of his people, which was to them as our Bible and prayer book are to us. And the story which that thoughtful priest put into the song was the story of the wren. And ever since that time so long ago, the song has been sung by the Pawnees and has been handed down from generation to generation.

THE LOST BABY AND THE UPLAND PLOVER

There is told among the people of the Dakota nation a very pretty and pathetic story of a lost baby. This story gives an intimate view of a feature in the old-time habits of life and means of subsistence among the prairie tribes. In early summer a busy occupation of the women was the harvesting of tipsin roots for the food supply of the family. The tipsin is a plant native on the high prairies. It is a species which belongs botanically to the bean family. Its roots are about the shape and size of a hen's egg, and they are of good food value and are very agreeable to the taste. The women, at the proper season in early summer, go out with their digging sticks to dig the tipsin roots, both for immediate use, and to preserve by drying for future use.

Of course a woman with a young infant must take it along with her when she goes out to this work, in order that she may take care of it and minister to its needs. While she is moving about over the prairie seeking tipsin plants, she places her baby, wrapped on its cradle-board, in some secure place till she can come back to it. Meantime she may wander widely over the prairie in her search of the plants.

The bird commonly called the upland plover is native on the high prairies where the tipsin abounds. The upland plover has a characteristic habit of flying up from the ground in the vicinity of its nest and hovering on outspread wings the while it utters a peculiarly vibrant, rather plaintive, trilling cry.

The story is that a young mother, taking her infant with her, had gone out alone on the prairie to dig tipsin roots. She laid the infant, wrapped on its cradle, in a safe place. Then she went about her work searching and digging tipsin roots. She continued her work for some time, wandering here and there over an extended area. After a while she looked for her babe, to take it up and give it care. The prairie looked alike everywhere. She went to a place where she thought she had left the baby, but she did not find it there. She looked farther and still could not find it. She was bewildered and frightened, half blinded by her tears, and weak with dismay and alarm. Now she approached a spot which she surely thought was the place where she had left her infant. Yes, there at a distance she saw some object slightly moving, which she thought was the cradle-wrapping fluttering in the prairie breeze. As she hastened toward the place, an upland plover rose into the air with its plaintive cry; but nowhere could she see anything of her baby. The plover's cry sounded to her like the cry of her infant, and it seemed to her that in some mysterious manner her baby had been changed into the bird and had flown away from her. Long she gazed after the bird and crooned endearing terms, but she could not call back her child. Thus her relatives found her when they came out to see what had kept her so long.

And the baby was seen no more, but the mother thought of it with grieving whenever afterward she heard the tremulous cry of the upland plover out on the prairie. And ever since, when people of the Dakota nation hear the plaintive call of the upland plover they are reminded of the young mother whose babe was mysteriously changed into that bird and how it flew away sadly crying.

SOCIETIES OF BIRDS

Some people of the Dakota nation used to think that certain kinds of birds formed societies and clubs among themselves, as human beings do. They held this opinion because they observed certain species of birds holding dances—for instance, the prairie chicken. From this observation, the Indians thought that the birds had customs similar to their own. They say that most kinds of birds have their own dances, which each kind conducts in its own way. They say that in some of their ways the prairie chicken and the meadow lark are similar. They also say that some kinds of birds speak human words, and that one kind which does so is the meadow lark.

In the springtime, after a rain, prairie chickens often hold a dance on a level place out on the prairie. In such a place, where the ground is smooth, the prairie chickens come together in a large number, like a crowd of people, and there they stand about close together. Presently one of the males steps into the circle of the group and dances, rattling his tail feathers, swelling out two orange-colored pouches on the sides of his neck. These pouches are like the bag of a bagpipe. As he swells out these bags, he makes a peculiar booming sound while he dances round and round, finally coming back to the place of starting. Then other males do likewise in turn. After a while they all pause as if to rest, and then they dance together again in the same manner as before, and so continue for about two hours; then they quit and disperse. They begin their dance just before sunrise and continue till a while after the sun is up.

The Indians say that at the time the prairie chickens are holding their dance they pay very little attention to a man even should he come near, and that even if he shoots at them with arrows, they take little notice of it, not flying away until they have finished their dance. But when that is over they fly away, all going their separate ways about their other affairs.

A man of the Dakota nation told of coming one time upon one of these prairie chicken dances on the prairie. He said that he came near and shot quite a number of the birds and that the others still went on dancing. He said that those which had been shot were flapping about on the ground and that the others seemed to think that these were still dancing. Finally those still living flew away, and then he picked up those he had shot and carried them home.

The meadow lark has a yellow breast with a mark in the center shaped like a crescent moon, so that it is said the breast of this bird looks like a sunflower. One of the great religious ceremonial dances of the Dakota nation is called the Sun Dance. They say that the meadow lark has a peculiar way of dancing like the Dakota Sun Dance. In the Dakota Sun Dance, the dancer dances steadily gazing toward the sun in a state of religious ecstasy. They say that thus singly the meadow larks dance, singing *Hiya-hehai!* in the manner of a dancer in the Sun Dance. It is said that meadow larks will often light upon a flat stone on the prairie and there dance in this manner, singing this cry of the Sun Dancer.

The people say that the meadow lark imitates the speech of human beings. They say that meadow larks come close to the dwellings of human beings at night and listen to what they say, and that next morning the larks mock the people, singing out what they have heard the night before. The Dakotas say that if you pay attention when the meadow lark sings, you can plainly distinguish words and sentences.

But they say that it is not only the meadow lark which thus sings words and sentences of human speech, but some other kinds of birds also do this. Two other kinds of birds which thus talk are the brown thrasher and the red-winged blackbird. They talk while they fly, and sometimes as they sit in the trees. Because of the habit the birds have of talking, the people listen attentively to hear what they will say. Some kinds of birds are very talkative. Every morning you can hear them warbling, and so they make the days very pleasant.

THE CAPTIVE BIRD

Indians in general do not think of humankind as being above and separate from all other creatures, but as fellow creatures in a world of life. The following incident, which took place many years ago on the prairies of Nebraska among a group of children of the Omaha tribe, will serve to show the attitude commonly held by Indians toward other forms of life. It might be well to repeat in this connection that Indian children were taught by their parents not to be wasteful and destructive of wild flowers, that they should not wantonly pluck them, for, they were told, if they did so, they would thus destroy the flower babies, and the flower nations would then be exterminated. Indians feel a fearful dread of the consequences of interfering with the nice balance and adjustment of nature.

It was a bright, warm summer afternoon in northern Nebraska. The wild grass, waving in the summer breeze, was like a shimmering emerald sea, flecked with varied color of the many different tribes of wild flowers. Overhead was a brilliantly blue sky with here and there slow-sailing white clouds, whose soft shadows came and passed, silent and entrancing, over the greenth of the prairie. And in all this scene the living creatures were moving, intent upon affairs of their own—the crickets and grasshoppers and the small mammals among the grass, the butterfly flitting from flower to flower, the antelopes grazing in groups, and now and then a hawk circling high overhead.

Across the prairie came a caravan of people with their camp equipage. A band of Omahas was on the summer buffalo hunt. The men were widely deployed in front and over a wide extent on both sides far in advance of the moving column. They were on the lookout for signs of the herd. When a herd should be sighted, the scouts who had found them would at once report to the officers. When the camp was made, the officers would confer and make plans for the "surround" and the kill.

The boys were employed in looking after the herd of extra horses; some of the women were with the train of pack animals, looking after the baggage and camp equipment; others were scattered over the prairie along the line of march, carrying digging sticks and bags to gather tipsin roots for food.

Groups of small children, too small to have any particular tasks assigned to them, were playing along the way, observing the ways of beasts and birds and insects, and admiring the brilliant wild flowers. One such group found a fledgling meadow lark, not yet able to fly. They captured it and brought it along with them when the band went into camp for the night. As the families sat about their tents waiting the preparation of the evening meal, the children showed their father the captive bird and told him 'how they caught it. He listened to their account and then told them something of the life and habits of the bird, its nesting and home life, its love of life and freedom, and its place in the world under the wise plans of Wakanda, Master of Life. He brought the children to see the unhappiness and the terror which they had unwittingly brought upon the captive and the anxiety the mother bird would feel over its loss.

Then he said to them: "Now children, take the little bird back to the place where you found it and set it down in the grass and say, 'O Wakanda, here is thy little bird which we have set free again. We are sorry that we took it away from its home and its people. We did not think of the sorrow we should cause. We wish to restore it and have it happy again with its people. May we be forgiven for our thoughtlessness; we will not do such wrong again.' "

The children carried out their father's instructions and placed the little bird again as near as they could to the place where they had captured it; and they recited the prayer to the Master of Life which their father had admonished them to say. As they returned to the camp, the quiet of the summer evening lay over all the land, the afterglow of the sunset was in the western sky, the white tents stood in a great circle upon the prairie, a twinkling campfire before each tent. The children were thoughtful. They had had a glimpse of the unity of the universe. They never forgot the lesson. Years passed; great changes came. The white people were coming into the land. Old activities and industries of the Indians were destroyed by the changes. The children of that little group went away from their people to attend the white men's schools, to learn the white men's ways and adapt themselves to those ways. But this did not cause them to forget altogether the wisdom and grace of their parental teaching. Long afterward they told this little story to the writer, who now gives it to you, reader, and wishes that you also may know that there be those in all lands and among all peoples who 'do justly, love mercy, and walk humbly with God.'

THE PLANT TRIBES

THE PRECIOUS GIFT OF CORN

All the tribes that cultivated corn had legends accounting for its acquisition. Many of these are very interesting and beautiful. In the sacred legends of the Omahas, of which account is given in "The Omaha Tribe," by Alice Fletcher and Francis La Flesche, in the Twenty-seventh Annual Report of the Bureau of American Ethnology, occurs the following legend of the finding of corn:

"Then a man in wandering about found some kernels, blue, and red, and white. He thought he had secured something of great value, so he concealed them in a mound. One day he thought he would go to see if they were safe. When he came to the mound he found it covered with stalks having ears bearing kernels of these colors. He took an ear of each kind and gave the rest to the people to experiment with. They tried it for food, found it good, and ever since have called it their life. As soon as the people found the corn good, they thought to make mounds like that in which the kernels had been hid. So they took the shoulder blade of an elk and built mounds like the first and buried the corn in them. So the corn grew and the people had abundant food."

While the legend does not designate what tribe it was which first obtained corn, it is probably to be identified with the following fuller account which is also told in the Omaha sacred legends, and which recites that they first learned of corn and obtained seed of it from the Arikaras. The story tells how the Arikaras first obtained corn by divine favor, and then how they gave it to other tribes, among these fortunate ones being the Omahas. It should be remembered that at the time when the Omahas came to the region where they now reside and have resided for some centuries, the Arikaras were in the region of what is now northern Nebraska, and so they were neighbors of the Omahas. No doubt the declaration of the legend that the Omahas did first obtain corn from the Arikaras is based on fact, in that corn culture among the Omahas had been borrowed from the Arikaras, who later migrated farther north along the upper Missouri River.

The story runs thus:

"The Arikaras were the first to obtain the maize. A young man went out hunting. He came to a high hill, and, looking down upon a valley, he saw a buffalo bull standing in the middle of a bottom land lying between two rivers at their confluence. As the young man searched the surroundings to find how he might approach the buffalo, he was impressed with the beauty of the landscape. The banks of the two rivers were low and well timbered. He observed that the buffalo stood facing north; he saw also that he could not approach from any side within bowshot. He thought that the only way to get a chance to shoot the buffalo would be to wait until the animal moved close to the bank of one of the rivers, or to the hills where there were ravines and shrubs. So the young man waited. The sun went down and the buffalo had not moved; the young man went home disappointed. He lay awake nearly all night brooding over his disappointment, for food had become scarce and the buffalo would have afforded a good supply. Before dawn the young man arose and hastened to the place where he had discovered the buffalo, to see whether the animal might be somewhere near, if it had moved. Just as he reached the summit of the hill where he was the day before, the sun arose, and he saw that the buffalo was in the same spot. But he noticed that it was now facing toward the east. Again the young man waited for the animal to move, but again the sun went down while the buffalo remained standing in the same spot. The hunter went home and passed another restless night. He started out again before dawn and came to the top of the hill just as the sun arose, and saw the buffalo in the same place still, but it had now turned to face the south. The young man waited and watched all day, but when darkness came he once more had to go away disappointed. He passed another sleepless night. His desire to secure game was mixed with curiosity to know why the buffalo should so persistently remain in that one spot without eating or drinking or lying down to rest. He rose upon the fourth morning before dawn, his mind occupied with this curiosity, and made haste to reach the hill to see if the buffalo still stood in the same place. Morning light had come when he arrived at the hill, and he saw that the buffalo was standing in exactly the same place, but had turned around to face the west. He was determined now to know what the animal would do; so he settled down to watch as he had throughout the three previous days. He now began to think that the animal was acting in this manner under the influence of some unseen power for some mysterious purpose, and that he, as well as the buffalo, was controlled by the same influence. Darkness again came upon him and the animal was still standing in the same position. The young man returned home, but he was kept awake all night by his thoughts and wondering what would come of this strange experience. He rose before dawn and hastened again to the mysterious scene. As he reached the summit of the hill, dawn spread across all the land. Eagerly he looked. The buffalo was gone! But just where the buffalo had been standing, there appeared something like a small bush. The young man now approached the spot with a feeling of curiosity and of awe, but also something of disappointment. As soon as he came near he saw that what had appeared from a distance like a small bush was a strange unknown plant. He looked upon the ground and saw the tracks of the buffalo; he observed that they turned from the north to the east, and to the south, and to the west; and in the center there was but one buffalo track, and out of it had sprung this strange plant. He examined the ground all around the plant to find where the buffalo had left the place, but there were no other footprints except those he had already seen near the plant. He made haste to reach his home village. There he notified the chiefs and elders of his people concerning the strange experience which he had had. Led by the young man, they proceeded to the place of the buffalo and examined the ground with care, and found that what he had told them was true. They found the tracks of the buffalo where he had stood and where he had turned, but could find no trace of his coming to the place nor of his going from it. Now while all these men believed that this plant had been given to the people in this mysterious manner by Wakanda for their use, still they were not sure what that use might be nor in what manner it should be used. The people knew of other plants that were useful for food, and the season for their ripening, and, believing that the fruit of this strange plant would ripen in its proper time, they arranged to guard and protect it carefully, awaiting with patience the time of its ripening and further revelation of its purpose.

"After a time a spike of flowers appeared at the top of the plant, but from their knowledge of other plants they knew that the blossom was but the flower and not the fruit. But while they watched this blossom, expecting it to develop into fruit, as they hoped it would, a new growth appeared from the joints of the plant. They now gave special attention to the new growth. It grew larger, and finally something appeared at the top which looked like hair. This, in the course of time, turned from pale green to dark brown, and after much discussion the people concluded that this growth at the side of the plant was its fruit, and that it had ripened. Until this time no one had dared to approach within touch of the plant. Although they were anxious to know the uses to which the plant could be put, or for which it was intended, no one dared to touch it. While the people were assembled around the plant, uncertain and undetermined how to approach the examination of it to learn its possible use, a youth stepped forward and spoke:

" 'Everyone knows how my life from childhood has been worse than useless, that my life among you has been more evil than good. Then, since no one would regret, should any evil befall me, let me be the first to touch this plant and taste of its fruit, so that you may not suffer any harm and that you may learn if the plant possesses qualities which may be for our good.'

"When the people gave their assent, the youth stepped forward and placed his hands over the top of the plant and brought them down by the sides of the plant to the roots in the manner of giving thanks and blessing. He then grasped the fruit, and, turning to the people, said, 'It is solid; it is ripe.' Very gently then he parted the husks at the top, and again turning to the people, he said, 'The fruit is red.' Then he took a few of the grains, showed them to the people, then ate them, and replaced the husks. The youth suffered no ill effects, and the people were convinced that this plant was given them for food. In the autumn, when the prairie grass had turned brown, the stalks and the leaves of this plant also turned brown. The fruit was plucked and put away with carefulness. The next spring the kernels were divided among the people, four to each family. The people removed to the place where the strange plant had appeared, and there they built their huts along the banks of the two rivers. When the hills began to be green from the new prairie grass, the people planted the kernels of this strange plant, having first built mounds like the one out of which the first plant grew. To the great joy of the people, the kernels sprouted and grew into strong, healthy plants. Through the summer they grew and developed, and the fruit ripened as did that of the original plant. The fruit was gathered, and some was eaten and was found to be good. In gathering the fruit the people discovered that there were various colors—some ears were white and others were blue, some were red, others were yellow.

"The next season the people gathered a rich harvest of this new plant. In the autumn these people, the Arikaras, sent invitations to a number of different tribes to come and visit them. Six tribes came; one of these was the Omaha. The Arikaras were very generous in the distribution of the fruit of this new plant among their guests, and in this manner a knowledge of the plant came to the Omahas."

VENERATION OF MOTHER CORN

The cultivation of corn was very closely and intimately interwoven into all the national life and thought of all the different Indian nations which practiced agriculture, and especially of the Arikaras and Pawnees, who had brought it northward with them in their migration into the region of the Missouri River from its original habitat in the tropical region. They looked upon corn as a divine gift, and they paid it becoming veneration in beautiful ritualistic ceremonies which were replete with poetic imagery and symbolism. In these religious ceremonies, corn was revered and honored; it was spoken of by the endearing and at the same time highly respectful title of "Mother Corn."

In an Arikara ceremony in honor of Mother Corn, there was given at a certain stage of the ritual a set address recalling to the minds of the people their debt to Mother Corn for her precious gift. Among other expressions, there occur words to the following effect:

In ancient time God sent Mother Corn to our people to be their friend and helper, to give them support and health and strength. Mother Corn has come to us out of the ancient time. She has walked with our people the long and difficult path which they have traveled from the far-away past; and now she marches with us toward the future. In the dim, distant days, Mother Corn gave food to our ancestors; and as she gave to them, so now she gives to us; and as to our forefathers and to us, so also she will be faithful and bountiful to our children. Now and in all time to come she will give to us the blessings for which we have prayed.

Mother Corn leads us as she has led our fathers all down the ages. The path of Mother Corn lies ahead, and we walk with her day by day, going forward with hope and confidence toward the future, just as our fathers followed her leading through all the past ages. When the lonely prairie stretched wide and fearful before us, we were doubtful and afraid; but Mother Corn strengthened and comforted us.

And now Mother Corn comes here making our hearts glad. Give thanks! She brings us a blessing. She brings peace and plenty. She comes to us from God who has given us good things.

The entire ceremony of the elaborate festival of Mother Corn was filled with reverent feeling and deep religious thought. The last act of the ceremony was in the quiet of evening, about sunset. The stalk of corn which had been before the altar throughout all the ceremony, there representing in visual form the spirit of Mother Corn, was now taken up and dressed like a woman and carried in religious procession down to the brink of the Mysterious River, which white men call the Missouri River, and piously consigned to the current of the stream, so that it might be carried back along the course of migration of the Arikara nation in their coming into this land, as a token of remembrance and affection from the present to the past.

The Mysterious River, the Holy River, has witnessed such scenes and ceremonies for ages past. In its valley and the valleys of its tributaries very many generations of people have toiled and tilled their crops with bone hoes, and have carried home their harvests in baskets upon their backs. In times of peace, happy travelers and traders have gathered on its shores for visiting and feasting and for trafficking in the fruits of the land. But at times wars have come between nations adjacent to the great river; and at such times it has witnessed war's terrors and desolation. The wooded ravines of its valley have served to hide the approach of enemies; the hills have resounded to the·shouts of battle.

So the Mysterious River, the Wonderful River, has been a powerful factor in shaping the activities and destinies of the Indian natives which have occupied its basin through many centuries past. Its course has been the great highway between north and south, and its tributaries have been the lines of travel between east and west. The course of this river has directed and facilitated the streams of migration of plant and animal life and of human population; it has been the avenue of exchange of useful material commodities, and of intellectual goods in human culture for many centuries before a white man ever saw it.

THE FRIENDLY CORN

It was summer. Most of the people of a Pawnee village were away from home on the summer buffalo hunt, but some had remained to tend the fields. Some of the fields were at a considerable distance from the village, at places where fertile soil was found in the little valley of some creek. These were too far away for the people conveniently to return home each night, and so they set up tents and camped near their fields for several days while they worked there.

In those days all good women tended their fields with loving care. It was said that "they lived with the corn." They diligently worked the soil about its roots, pulled out the weeds, and guarded it from crows and blackbirds and marauding animals. They tended and watched their corn lovingly, as a mother cherishes her children.

Two women were thus camped at the edge of their field. Night had fallen, and the women had retired to rest from their toil. The gentle night wind softly rustled the grasses and the leaves of the trees, with restful, murmuring sounds. The women fell asleep. Presently one of them awoke. It seemed to her that she heard low voices talking outside. At first she could not distinguish any words. She listened a while, and then she wakened her companion.

"Hark," she said, "do you not hear talking outside?"

But her companion was drowsy and indifferent. Both again slept. But the first woman was again wakened by the sound of low murmuring voices. Again she woke her companion and told her she was sure that she heard voices. Her companion was ill-disposed at being awakened, and said impatiently:

"Now I hope you will listen well and hear what is said if anyone is talking, and not continue waking me on account of your fancies."

Then she went to sleep again. But the first woman listened, and again it seemed to her that she really heard soft voices talking together in the corn-field as the night breeze rustled the corn blades.

As the woman listened intently, she finally could distinguish the words which were said, and she found that it was the corn plants talking among themselves. One was saying:

"Stretch yourselves and grow tall. Soon, now, our people will return to the village, and they will bring plenty of meat and fat of the buffalo. They will rejoice to see us again, and so they will burn for us some of the best of the meat and the fat to make smoke for us, so that we shall be glad. This they will do because of their love for us."

So it is that ever since that time it has been customary, when the people returned from the hunt, for the women to go out to their fields and visit their corn, and to make a burnt offering of some of the best of the meat and the fat which they had brought home from the hunt. While away on the hunt, preparing the meat to bring home, they made selection of some of the best for this purpose, to make the corn glad.

When the people returned from the summer hunt they always went out to visit their fields to see how the corn had prospered while they had been away. When they found the corn flourishing, they rejoiced and were glad to see it again, as they would be at seeing members of their own family after an absence. But if it chanced that they found their beloved corn damaged by an enemy, or seared by drouth, or beaten and battered by hail, or ruined by a devouring host of grasshoppers, then they suffered pain and grief, as from the misfortune of their own relatives.

When they returned home and found the new corn ready for eating, they did not pluck it at once. Such action would be greedy and impious. First there was public worship and thanksgiving at the holy lodge. And then, after the public worship, the people gladly resorted to their fields and gathered of the new corn and feasted and made merry with their friends and extended hospitality to any strangers who might be visitors at their village.

THE FORGOTTEN EAR OF CORN

A woman of the Arikara tribe was harvesting her crop of corn, making ready to store it away in a safe place where she might be able to get it for use during the long cold winter. She went along gathering the ears and placing them in convenient heaps so that she could gather them up to carry to the storage place she had prepared. When she had finished her work she started to go, but she heard a voice like the voice of a little child, crying and calling pitifully,

"Oh, do not leave me! Do not go away without me."

The woman was astonished at what she supposed was the voice of a lost child. She said to herself,

"What is this? Can it be that some child has wandered and has been lost in my cornfield? I must go and look for it."

So she laid down her burden of gathered corn and went back into the field to make search. But she found no child anywhere in the field.

Then she started once more to take up her burden and leave the field. But again she heard the plaintive little voice crying,

"Oh, do not leave me! Do not go away without me."

Then she went back into the field and searched again for a long time. After diligent search, she found one little ear of corn which had been covered by stalks and leaves. It was the little ear of corn which had been crying, fearing to be left to die in the field. So all Indian women are very careful in gathering their crops, that nothing shall be lost or wasted of the good gifts of the Great Mystery, for they are accounted sacred and holy, and it would be wicked to treat them with neglect or indifference.

SACRED TREES

A people living under natural conditions, in communion with nature, will carefully note the appearance of natural objects in their environment. They become acquainted with the various aspects of the landscape and of the living things—plants and animals—in their changes through the seasons, in storm and calm, in activity and in repose. Becoming thus intimately acquainted with the life about them, the people will come to regard some of the more notable forms with a feeling akin to that which they have toward persons, and hence animals and plants come to have place in folk stories, in reasoned discourse, and in ceremonies of religion.

Commonly throughout the region of the Missouri River was to be seen the cottonwood, the willows of several species, and the cedar or juniper. The appearance and habits of these trees impressed themselves powerfully upon the mind and imagination of the Indian folk.

The cedar or juniper was wonderful because it was ever green; unlike other trees, it appeared indifferent to frost and to heat, but alike in winter and summer retained its leaves. Also it appeared to be withdrawn, solitary and silent, standing dark and still, like an Indian standing upon a hill in prayer and meditation, with his robe drawn over his head. Thus it gave the suggestion and had the appearance of being in communion with the High Powers.

Leaves and twigs of cedar were burned as incense in ceremonial rituals in order that evil influences might be driven away.

Willows were always found growing along watercourses, as though they had some duty or function in the world in connection with water, the element so immediately and constantly needful to man and to all other living things. Water was not only imperatively necessary for vivifying and reanimating all living things, but was an active agent in processes of change and transmutation. In cases of disease, the evil influences which plagued the body might be driven out, and thus health might be restored, through the use of water transformed into vapor by means of heat. So the vapor bath was used. Also, if a man contemplated the undertaking of any serious project, any dangerous mission, or any solemn enterprise, it was important first to prepare himself by purification, by means of the vapor bath, from all evil influences. The framework of the vapor bath lodge was made of willow poles, bent and tied with their bark.

The willow was also mystically connected with that greatest change of all, the departure of the spirit from the body, the change which we call death. Willow twigs had certain uses in funeral rites.

The cottonwood was found growing over a widely extended range, under diverse climatic conditions, appearing always self-reliant, showing prodigious fecundity, and having wonderful means of propagation. It provided its seeds, produced in enormous number, with a device by which they traveled on the wind to far places and so became widely disseminated in all directions, traveling upstream or downstream, and even across the plains and prairies to other streams where the new generation might establish itself. But besides this admirable provision to insure the perpetuation of its kind, it had also another means of propagation, though by this means it could move only downstream. This method of propagation is by the making of cuttings or slips from its own twigs. It is well known that the gardener may make artificial cuttings of many kinds of trees and plants, and so may increase his stock. But the cottonwood, alone among trees, performs this operation itself. At the beginning of autumn the cottonwood trees form layers of cork cells which gradually wedge off part of a twig from its parent branch, thus covering and healing the wound of separation and also covering and healing the base of the separated twig, so that it falls off alive and protected from loss of sap.

Falling thus to the ground just about the time that autumn rains are about to begin, the slips are ready to be carried away by the rising waters of the streams and may be thus planted in a mud or sand bank farther downstream, ready to take root and grow in the springtime.

In the springtime, the opening of the cottonwood buds and the pushing out of young leaves even when chilly nights follow the bright breezy days, and the rapid growth of these lustrous leaves, brightly dancing in the spring winds, their brilliant sheen and active movement reflecting the splendor of the sun like the dancing, glinting ripples of a lake, suggest the joy and eagerness and energy of movement of all returning life.

The foliage of the cottonwood is peculiar and remarkable; the air is never so still that there is not motion of cottonwood leaves. Even in still and sultry summer afternoons, and at night when all else was still, ever the Indians could hear the rustling of cottonwood leaves by the passage of little vagrant currents of air. Secret messages seemed ever to be passing in soft whispers among the cottonwood leaves. And the winds themselves are the bearers of the messages and commands of the Higher Powers; so there was constant reminder of the mystic character of this tree.

The cottonwood was, among trees, the symbol of fidelity, one of the great virtues inculcated by the ethical code of the people of the Dakota nation.

From all these considerations it might be expected that this tree should have an important place in the rituals of the people for many generations associated with it. And so it had.

The Sacred Pole of the Omaha nation was made of the cottonwood. The Sacred Pole was an object of the greatest veneration to that people, as the Ark of the Covenant was sacred to the Hebrews.

The Sacred Tree, the central object of the Sun Dance, the most momentous religious ritual of the Dakota nation, is a cottonwood. The tree chosen to be felled and brought into camp and set up in the lodge erected for the performance of this ritual must be a growing cottonwood tree, the base of whose trunk is not less than two spans in circumference. The tree must be straight to a distance from the ground of about four times the measure of the outstretched arms from hand to hand, where it must be forked.

Twigs and bark of cottonwood were burned as incense to ward against the scheming of Anog Ité, the spiteful, malevolent being who foments scandals, strife and infidelity.

Such, then, are some of the relations in the philosophic thought, the religious conceptions and the sentiments of the people of several Indian nations in regard to these three species of trees.

GRANDMOTHER CEDAR TREE

In every country and at all times, geographic features, such as mountains, plains, valleys, rivers, lakes and seas, have greatly influenced the lives of men and nations. We see notable examples of such influence in the river Nile in Egypt and the Danube and the Rhine in Europe. Likewise in North America the St. Lawrence River, the Great Lakes and the Mississippi River and its tributaries, the Ohio and the Missouri, have had great influence in determining the movements and shaping the activities of men. Not only have these lakes and rivers of North America influenced the lives of people in our times, but so they influenced the lives of the people of the tribes and nations of Indians who were here before us.

Two nations, the Pawnees and the Arikaras, came into the Great Plains from the southwest, from the borders of Mexico, and gradually in the course of centuries moved northward to the Missouri River.

They moved along the course of this river, the Arikaras always in advance, until at last this tribe came to live in what is now North Dakota, while the Pawnees still remained in the country which is now called Nebraska.

Both the Arikaras and the Pawnees named this river the Holy River, or Mysterious River, because it meant so much to them. It was to them their River of Life. The river was closely connected with their sacred legends and religious rituals. All along the course of the Missouri River from Nebraska even up to the present location of the Arikaras in North Dakota, remains may be seen of ancient villages of that nation. All these sites have been successively occupied and abandoned by the Arikaras in their age-long northward migration. But these ancient seats of their ancestors are not forgotten. The Arikaras of the present day sometimes visit them and often think of them and of the past life of their people when they lived there.

The Sacred Legend of the Arikaras, which is the unwritten Bible of that nation, has been passed down by word of mouth by faithful priests from generation to generation for many centuries. It tells of the beginnings of life upon the earth, and of the gradual progress from confusion to order, of the advancement of all forms of life from crude beginnings to ever higher attainments toward perfection. It teaches that all things in the living world, every species of plant or animal, from the humblest to the proudest, has its proper place in the scheme of perfection; that all are kin; that none should be despised, for the lack or loss of any one would detract from the completeness and harmony of the whole. It tells of the final appearance of humankind upon the earth, brother and friend to all the forms that had already appeared. It tells of the pitiful hardships of life experienced by the first human beings: they were poor and needy; they had to learn by hard experience how to live in the world, how to shelter themselves from storms and defend themselves from dangers; they had to learn also by trial and bitter experience how to provide themselves with food, what things were good and wholesome and what were harmful.

In their bewilderment the first human beings were comforted and encouraged by a friendly Voice bidding them welcome into the world of living things. By and by they came to know that this friendly Voice which spoke to them was the Voice of Vegetation giving them friendly greeting. Again, when the people were discouraged and distressed, ill and in need, and buffeted by the strong winds and cruel storms, the Voice was heard speaking to them, telling them to lay hold upon the cedar and it would help them. They heeded the counsel of the Voice and besought the cedar. The cedar comforted them and promised to help and protect them. So they had rest and quiet from the storm in the shelter of the cedar trees, for the cedar was very strong, and able to withstand all the angry gusts of stormy wind. And cedar leaves and twigs are used for incense and also for medicine. So, as a mark of gratitude, the cedar is called Grandmother and a religious ceremony, called the Ceremony of Holy Grandmother Cedar Tree, is performed every year.

The veneration of the Holy Cedar Tree is in effect an act of worship of the principle or essence of Life, a cedar tree being employed as a symbol of Everlasting Life. A cedar tree is brought in from the place where it grew in the wilderness and placed on the prairie at a certain distance from the holy lodge, the tribal temple. The priests go out to this place and there set up the tree and consecrate it. Then it is again taken up and carried in religious procession upon the shoulders of the bearers to the sacred lodge. When they come into the temple yard, they let the tree down from their shoulders, and the people gladly rush forward, bearing gifts which they lay upon the tree. The priests give blessing to the donors. It is a time of rejoicing and good feeling among the people. Later, at the conclusion of the ceremonies, these gifts are distributed to the poor and unfortunate in the tribe. The bearers again take the tree upon their shoulders, carrying it in procession into the tribal temple or sacred lodge. After the ceremonies within the lodge are concluded, the tree is carried out and erected in front of the lodge. There the tree stands as a witness and participant with the people in the later celebration of the festival to Mother Corn, and in all their joys and sorrows during the remainder of the summer, through the following autumn and winter. So it remains with the people until the end of winter has come, when the ice has gone out of the river and the pasque flowers again bring their cheering promise of coming spring.

Then the people come together on a day when the message of returning spring has come again. They fasten to the branches of the cedar tree the worn-out moccasins of their little children. Now they take up the tree again and carry it in religious procession down to the Mysterious River, which white people call the Missouri River, and consign it to the current of the stream, so that it may drift down past all the old Arikara village sites, carrying to them the message that the Arikara nation still lives, that the people still remember and revere the wise teachings and good precepts of the ancients, and that they still have hope for the future, as attested by the little moccasins, worn by the baby feet of the oncoming generation. Besides the baby moccasins, symbolic of the hope and promise of continuity of the tribe, they also sometimes attach to the branches of the Holy Cedar Tree the blossoms of the pasque flower, which are just coming into bloom at that time, symbolic of the promise of returning springtime and the reawakening of all forms of life to renewed activity and to triumph over the death and darkness and cold of winter.

TIPSIN

Over all the dry prairies of the Great Plains region there grows a plant which was an important item of the food supplies of all the tribes of the region. It is a species which belongs botanically to the bean family. The part used for food is the large root, which is about the size of a hen's egg. The stem of the plant is bushy and branched; the leaves are trifoliate. The leaves and stem of the plant are hairy, giving it a grayish-green appearance. The flowers are set in close racemes at the ends of the branches, and are bluish in color and of the shape of bean blossoms.

In the journals of the early travelers, mention of this plant is often found under the name of "pomme blanche" or "pomme de prairie," the name by which the French traders and trappers called it, for they learned from the Indians to live upon the native products of the land. English-speaking people, coming later and depending not so much on native products, did not supply names for them, not considering them of enough importance. The name which I have given to this plant for a common English name is an approximation to, and an adaptation of, its name in the Dakota language.

When the seeds of the tipsin plant have ripened, the top of the plant breaks off at the surface of the ground and goes rolling over the prairie, driven by the winds. Thus the seeds are scattered. In this way nature provides for the dissemination of the species. After the top of the plant has broken off and blown away, there is nothing left by which the location of the root can be found. Therefore it is necessary for the people to make the harvest of the tipsin roots while they can still be found, before the tops have been blown away. So, while the plants are in bloom and afterwards, so long as the tops are still in place, showing the location of the roots, the women are busy improving the opportunity to harvest as large a supply as possible of this good food.

For future use the roots are peeled and dried for preservation, but they are also used while fresh. They are cooked by stewing with meat or with dried green corn. For drying, either the roots were sliced into pieces and spread to dry in the sun and air, or the peeled roots entire were braided together into strings and hung up thus to dry.

The women gathered the roots by digging them out of the sod by means of digging sticks. The mothers had to look after their children, of course, and so they often had to take the children with them out upon the prairie when they went out to dig tipsin roots. In order to keep the children interested and occupied, the mothers would let them help in the work. Of course the children could not do the heavy work of digging the roots out of the tough prairie sod, but their sharp eyes could spy out the plants among the grass. This the children were delighted to do, for it made them feel as though they were of some importance and were doing something worth while, as indeed they were. Thus the Indian children early and pleasantly learned to take part in necessary tasks and to acquire useful knowledge and to have assurance and ability in self-support.

When they went out to the prairie to dig tipsin roots, the mothers would show the children some of the plants and call attention to their appearance and habits. Noting the branching form of these plants, the mother would say to the children: "See, they point to each other. Now here is one: notice the directions in which its arms are pointing. If you go along in these directions and look closely you will find other plants in line with the direction of each pointing arm."

The children were interested and eager to show their own alertness and ability, and so they were happily busy in finding other tipsin plants for their mothers to dig. Of course, if the children followed any of these lines and kept close watch they would soon find another plant. The pretty fancy of the plants pointing to each other stimulated the lively interest of the children. Thus they made a pleasing game of their work.

THE GROUND BEAN AND THE
BEAN MOUSE

Besides the plants which Indians cultivated in their fields and gardens for their food supply, they also made use of many uncultivated wild plants. One of the native plants which was of much importance as a food plant is a wild bean which grows over a very extensive area of North America. This plant is interesting from its peculiar natural history, and especially because of its relation to the economic life of all the different nations of Indians in whose countries it grew. We call it commonly the "ground bean." In the Dakota language, this plant is called *maka ta omnica,* which means "bean of the earth." In the Pawnee language, it is called *ati-kuraru,* which means "earth bean."

From the important place which the ground bean held in the food supply of the tribes, and the interesting and unique manner in which it was obtained, it figures largely in the folklore of the region in which it thrives. Strangely enough, white people have never investigated its usefulness nor its possibilities of improvement under cultivation and selective breeding.

Many early travelers and explorers mention the use of the ground bean by Indians, but almost all of them are uncertain of the nature and identity of the plant and of the animal which harvests it.

The scientific name of the ground bean is *Falcata*

comosa; it is popularly called ground bean from its habit of producing one form of its fruits in the ground, as the peanut grows. The plant forms two kinds of branches, bearing two forms of flowers, producing two forms of fruits. Leafy branches climb up over shrubs, or, in the absence of support, form a tangled mass of vines. Upon these leafy branches are borne showy purplish flowers exactly resembling garden-bean blossoms, but very much smaller. From these small flowers on the upper branches are produced small bean pods, about half an inch to an inch in length, which contain each from three to five small mottled beans about an eighth of an inch long.

From the base of the main stem of the plant the branches of the second form grow out in all directions, creeping prostrate on the ground under the shade of the overgrowth and forming a perfect network of colorless, leafless branches. The tiny, inconspicuous blossoms borne on these prostrate branches are self-pollinated and push into the leaf mold and soft soil, where each produces a single large bean closely invested in a filmy pod or husk. These beans are about the size of lima beans, or even larger. They are ivory white, beautifully and variously mottled with red and purple. It is these large ones which are so good for food and so greatly desired. When cooked, they are of excellent flavor. But these desirable beans would be difficult to obtain were it not for the help of a certain species of small mammal (*Microtus pennsylvanicus*), commonly called meadow mouse, or bean mouse. These mice gather great stores of food for winter—certain roots and seeds, and most especially the ground beans. It is from this activity that the animal is called bean mouse. The mice hollow out storage places in the ground, where they put away their winter supplies.

When we speak of this little animal as a mouse, calling it bean mouse, we must not think of it as we think of the house mouse. The house mouse is a filthy little thief and is therefore everywhere detested. But the bean mouse is a cleanly, orderly, hard-working and provident little animal. Because it is orderly, and because it does lay up provisions for future use, Indians call it a "civilized mouse," in contrast to some other species of animals which live from day to day on whatever they can find, laying up no stores. Species of animals which live in this haphazard way they speak of as "uncivilized," in contrast to the bean mice which are observed to live in an orderly and respectable manner.

These stores of ground beans were eagerly sought by Indians of all tribes throughout the range of the plant, and they were grateful to the bean mouse for harvesting and storing the ground beans. But the Indians said they must not take away all the beans from the stores of the bean mice, for it would be wicked to loot their stores and leave them destitute. They believed that if one were so hard-hearted and unjust as to do so, the action would surely bring due punishment.

The Indians said that when they went to seek the stores of beans laid up by the bean mice they must first prepare themselves in heart and mind. One must go on such a quest in all humility and charity, not only toward all humankind, but with a feeling of acknowledgment of the rights of all living things, plants and animals as well as human beings, and with a becoming sense of the interdependence of all living things. One must have a consciousness of one's debt to all nature and to all the Mysterious Powers. One going on this quest must, as they said, "think only good thoughts and have a good heart; one must put away any grudge or hard feelings. And especially we should think," they said, "of our debt to the bean mouse for the favor about to be asked of it." Thus they approached the stores of the bean mouse, not as robbers of the weak and helpless, but humbly asking of the little animal a portion of its stores for their own need.

THE USEFULNESS OF WILD RICE

Wenibozho of the Chippewas and his grandmother, Nokomis, lived together in a lodge by themselves. When he approached manhood his grandmother exhorted him to exert himself, to learn to endure hardship, loneliness, cold and hunger and thirst, for such experience is the proper training for a young man. A young man needs such training so that when overtaken by misfortune he shall be brave and resourceful, so that he may be able to take care of himself and of any who may be dependent upon him.

So one day Wenibozho told his grandmother he was going away into the wilderness where he had never been before, so that he could be cast upon his own resources to try his strength and courage and wit.

He was gone many days and nights, wandering through the forest and beside streams and lakes. He subsisted upon such fruits, seeds, roots and tubers as he was able to find, and upon the flesh of animals he was able to shoot with his bow and arrows which he had brought with him. One day he came to a lake in which was growing a great quantity of beautiful, feathery wild rice, swaying over the water in the gentle breeze. From the bark of a birch tree he fashioned a canoe in which he rowed out upon the lake and gathered a quantity of the wild rice. He did not know the wild rice was useful for food, for he had never seen it before, but he admired its beauty. He took to his grandmother the wild rice which he had gathered. He told her that he had found this beautiful plant in the lake and that he had brought to her some of the seed of the plant. This seed they sowed in another lake, near the place where they lived, for Wenibozho hoped to have the plant growing where he might often enjoy its beauty.

Again he went away into the forest so that he might become accustomed to endure hardships and also that he might learn wisdom from the living creatures—not only from the moving creatures but also from those other living creatures, the plants of all kinds. While walking he thought he heard a voice saying, "Sometimes they eat us." He stopped and listened and again he heard the words, "Sometimes they eat us." This time he perceived that the words came from some bushes near which he was passing. Finally he spoke, saying, "To whom are you talking?" He was told that he was the one to whom the bush was speaking; so he dug up the plant and found that it had a long root. He tasted the root, and it was pleasant to the taste; so he dug more and ate a great many—so many that he was made ill. He was too ill to travel, and so he lay there three days. Finally he was able to rise and move on, but he was hungry and weak. As he passed along, other plants spoke to him, but he was now afraid to eat of them. Then as he was walking along a stream he saw some bunches of grass growing up out of the water, which beckoned to him and said, "Sometimes they eat us." He was so hungry, and the graceful grass was so tempting, that he was constrained to gather some seeds of it and eat. The taste was pleasing, and its effect upon his hunger was so gratifying that he said, "O, you are indeed good! What are you called?" The grass replied, "We are called 'manomin,'" which is the name by which the Chippewa people call this plant. Wenibozho waded out into the water and gathered the grains by handfuls and ate it, and so continued till his hunger was fully satisfied. From eating the manomin he suffered no ill effects whatever, but was strengthened wonderfully. Finally he remembered the grain which he had discovered on his former journey and which he and his grandmother, Nokomis, had sown in the lake near their home. When he returned and found it growing and compared it with this grain which he had now found to be so good, he perceived that it was the same sort. So he found that this beautiful grass which he had growing in the lake near home was really manomin, as pleasant to the taste and as satisfying to hunger as it was beautiful to the eyes. Ever since that time the Chippewas have known how to value the good gift of manomin.

THE ARIKARA SILVERBERRY DRINK

Once on a time there was famine among the Arikaras. The people were sorely in want of food and of other comforts of life. Drought and frosts had destroyed their crops, so that their fields supplied but a very scant harvest. Because of the drought, the animals which the Arikaras ordinarily used for meat had gone far away. The late spring frosts had killed the blossoms of the wild fruit trees, so that now, when it was time for fruit, there was none. And the drought had so diminished the growth of the wild vegetation, as well as of their cultivated crops, that the people were able to obtain but meager quantities of edible seeds, roots, and tubers of wild plants. The little children often cried from hunger. The people were in pitiful condition. The men were making every endeavor, and every day they made painful and toilsome journeys in search of sustenance for their people.

One day a party of men were out on such an expedition, searching for anything which would furnish some comfort for their people. These men were weary, hungry, thirsty, and miserable. Upon a hill, from which they could see far around them over the country, they sat down upon the ground, and while here resting they heard a voice calling to them, saying, "You men upon the hill, come you down here!" The men looked at one another in doubt and anxiety, and with some fear because of this strange voice. Finally one of the men dared to go down in response to the call. He went to the place on the north slope of the hill whence the voice seemed to come, and there found himself standing in the midst of a scattered thicket of bushes with silver-gray leaves. "It was a clump of the bushes which our people call *nátara-kapáchis*, but which white people call silverberries," the Arikaras say. Now, as the man stood amid the bushes, he heard the voice again, saying to him, "I know your troubles and sorrows. I know the pitiful condition of your people. I have been wishing for you to come, so that I might do something for you. I have not much to offer, but what I have I shall be glad to give you for your comfort and for the comfort of your suffering people. Take some of my leaves and steep them in hot water. You will find they make a comforting hot drink."

The man took of the leaves as he was directed, and went back to his companions and told them what the voice had said. They steeped the leaves as they had been told, and found they made a pleasant drink. They were cheered and encouraged by the friendliness shown them by the silverberry bushes.

When the men came home to their people, they brought with them some of the leaves of the silverberry, and they told the people of the divine gift and showed them how to use these leaves. The people were thankful for the gift from the bushes, and were cheered and their hearts were strengthened by the kindness and friendliness which the silverberry bushes had thus shown to them. In token of the people's gratitude the priests performed a ceremony of thanksgiving and made smoke offerings to all the divine powers of the four quarters of the universe, to Mother Earth and to God above.

THE PRAIRIE ROSE

The prairie was gray and drab, no beautiful flowers brightened it, it had only dull greenish-gray herbs and grasses, and Mother Earth's heart was sad because her robe was lacking in beauty and brightness. Then the Holy Earth, our mother, sighed and said: "Ah, my robe is not beautiful, it is somber and dull. I wish it might be bright and beautiful with flowers and splendid with color. I have many beautiful, sweet and dainty flowers in my heart. I wish to have them upon my robe. I wish to have upon my robe flowers blue like the clear sky in fair weather. I wish also to have flowers white like the pure snow of winter and like the high white cloudlets of a quiet summer day. I wish also to have brilliant yellow flowers like the splendor of the sun at noon of a summer day. And I wish to have delicate pink flowers like the color of the dawn light of a joyous day in springtime. I would also have flowers red like the clouds at evening when the sun is going down below the western edge of the world. All these beautiful flowers are in my heart, but I am sad when I look upon my old dull gray and brown robe."

Then a sweet little pink flower said, "Do not grieve, mother. I will go up upon your robe and beautify it." So the little pink flower came up from the heart of Mother Earth to be upon the sad prairie of her mother's robe.

Now, when the Wind Demon saw the pink flower there, he said, "Indeed she is pretty, but I will not have her trespassing in my playground." So the Wind Demon rushed at her, shouting and roaring, and blew out her life, but her spirit returned to the heart of Mother Earth.

And when the other flowers ventured, one after another, to come out upon the prairie, which was

Mother Earth's robe, the Wind Demon destroyed them also, and their spirits returned to the heart of Holy Mother Earth.

At last Prairie Rose offered to go and brighten the appearance of Mother Earth's robe, the prairie. Mother Earth said fondly, "Yes, dear, sweet child, I will let you go. You are so lovely and your breath is so sweet, it may be that the Wind Demon will be charmed by you, and that he will let you remain on his ground." And Prairie Rose said, "Yes, dear mother, I will go, for I desire that my mother's robe shall be beautiful. But if the Wind Demon should blow out my life, my spirit shall return home to the heart of my mother."

So Prairie Rose made the toilsome journey up through the dark ground and came out upon the sad gray prairie. And as she was going, Mother Earth said in her heart, "Oh, I hope the Wind Demon will allow her to live, for I wish my robe to be beautiful!"

Now, when the Wind Demon saw Prairie Rose, he rushed at her, shouting, and said, "Indeed, though she is pretty, I shall not allow her to be upon my ground. I will blow out her life." So he came on, roaring and drawing his breath in strong gusts. Just then he caught the fragrance of the breath of Prairie Rose. "Ah," he said, "how sweet her breath is! Why, I do not have it in my heart to blow out the life of such a beautiful little maiden whose breath is so sweet! I love her. She shall stay here with me. And I must make my voice gentle and sing a melodious song, for I wish not to frighten her with my awful noise."

So he became quiet and breathed gentle breezes which passed over the prairie grasses whispering and humming little songs of gladness.

Then the other flowers also came up through the dark ground and out upon the dull gray prairie and made it bright and joyous with their presence. And the wind came to love all the flowers and the grasses.

And so the robe of our Mother Earth became beautiful because of the loveliness and the sweet breath of the Prairie Rose.

Sometimes the Wind forgets his gentle songs and becomes loud and boisterous, but he does not harm a person whose robe is ornamented with the color of Prairie Rose.

THE SUNFLOWER

Once on a time, long ago, a company of Dakota men were going upon a war expedition. And now, as they were within the country of the enemy, they were proceeding very cautiously. One morning very early, they heard what seemed to be the sound of someone singing in a tremulous voice, coming from the direction toward which they were marching. They stopped and stood still to listen.

As they stood thus listening, it seemed to them that the singer, whoever he might be, must be a clown, for he was singing a clown song. There was not light enough to see the singer. But they waited, silently and anxiously peering ahead in the direction from which came the sound of the singing. At the first glimmer of the dawn light they were able to make out the appearance of a man walking with an awkward shuffling gait. His robe was ragged and his leggings drooped down slouchingly in wrinkles about his ankles as he walked. He had circles about his eyes painted a bright yellow, and he was singing a clown song in a husky, wheezy voice.

So they stood wondering at the clown who was coming toward them. He was coming toward the rising sun, and as the daylight grew brighter they were astonished to see the man suddenly changed to a sunflower.

And ever since that time, it is said, the sunflower faces toward the sun.

THE SPIDERWORT

The spiderwort is a beautiful native prairie flower which is known under numerous popular names. It is called spiderwort, spider lily, ink flower, king's crown and various other names. It has been proposed to add to the list another name, "flower-of-romance." This name is proposed from the circumstance of a bit of pleasing sentiment connected with this flower in the folklore of the Dakota nation of Indians.

It is a charmingly beautiful and delicate flower,

deep blue in color, with a tender-bodied plant of graceful lines. There is no more appealingly beautiful flower on the western prairies than this one when it is sparkling with dewdrops in the first beams of the rising sun. There is about it a suggestion of purity, freshness and daintiness.

When a young man of the Dakota nation is in love and walking alone on the prairie finds this flower blooming, he stops and sings to it a song in which he personifies it with the qualities of his sweetheart's personality as they are called to his mind by the appearance of the flower before him, its characteristics figuratively suggesting the characteristics of her whose image he carries romantically in his mind and heart. In his mind the beauties of the flower and the charms of the girl are mutually transmuted and flow together into one image.

The words of his song, translated from the Dakota language into the English, are something like this:

> Tiny, gladsome flower,
> So winsome and modest,
> Thou art dainty and sweet.
> For love of thee I'd die.

THE SONG OF THE PASQUE FLOWER

The pasque flower has a very extensive range upon the northern prairies, reaching from about 43 degrees north latitude to the Great Slave Lake, above 60 degrees north latitude. It is the earliest flower to put forth its blossoms in the springtime, often appearing before all the snow is gone. Its bluish, lavender-colored flowers gladden the bare brown hillsides with great profusion of bloom, an earnest of returning life. For this reason it has a strong hold upon the affections of all the native tribes throughout all its extended range. The plant is closely related to the anemone, which is sometimes called the windflower.

The people of the Dakota nation have a number of pretty little folk stories concerning the pasque flower. One story is that in the long ago, whenever any of the people happened to pass by where these flowers were blooming, the flowers tried to show the friendliness which they felt for human beings by nodding their heads in the chilly spring wind, showing their smiling faces and saying, "Good morning! Good morning!" But the people passed them unheeding. The flowers became abashed at this indifference, and so nowadays, still feeling friendly towards the people in spite of such rebuffs, they bashfully turn their heads to one side as they nod and call their kindly greetings in their sweet low voice.

There is another pretty conceit connected with the pasque flower. Indians generally are keenly observant of all things in nature, and reverent towards them. They feel reverence for all living creatures, whether plant or animal. They have songs and stories about many of the species of plants and animals with which they are acquainted, such a song being the expression of the life or soul of the species to which it pertains. The song of the pasque flower, translated out of the Dakota language into English runs something like this:

I wish to encourage the children of other flower nations
Which are now appearing over all the land;
So, while they waken from sleep and rise from the bosom
Of Mother Earth, I stand here, old and gray-headed.

The saying, "I wish to encourage the children of other flower nations," refers to the very early pre-vernal blossoming of this plant and its consequent ripening while the other flower species (nations) are just peeping through the ground. The entire plant is hairy, and when mature its seed head is plumose and white, similar to the clematis head, suggesting the head of a very old man with long white hair. This explains the allusion in "I stand here, old and gray-headed."

When in springtime an old man of the Dakota nation first finds one of these flowers, it reminds him of his childhood, when he wandered over the hills at play as free from sorrow and care as the birds and the flowers. He sits down near the flower, upon the lap of Mother Earth, and takes out his pipe and fills it with tobacco. Then he reverently holds the pipe towards the earth, then towards the sky, then in turn towards the four quarters of the horizon. After this act of silent invocation and thanksgiving, he

smokes. Tobacco was sacred and was used ceremonially as an incense. The pipe was therefore a
sort of censer, and was accordingly treated with respect and reverence. In smoking, Indians did not
seize the pipestem in the teeth. Such an act would
be sacrilegious. The mouthpiece of the pipestem
was gently presented to the lips and the breath was
drawn through. By this inspiration the smoker
united the mystery of the tobacco, the mystery of
fire and the mystery of the breath of life.

While the old man sits by the flower and smokes,
he meditates upon all the changing scenes of his lifetime—his joys and sorrows, his youthful hopes, his
accomplishments, his disappointments, and the guidance of the Unseen Powers accorded to him thus far
upon the journey of life—and he is encouraged to
believe that he will be guided to the end of life's
journey, "beyond the fourth hill" of life. As he has
been guided over the hill of childhood, the hill of
youth, and the hill of manhood's prime, so he will
also be guided over the last hill, the hill of old age.

After finishing his pipe, he empties the ashes
reverently upon the ground near the pasque flower
which he has been contemplating. Then he rises and
plucks the flower prayerfully and carries it carefully
home to show to his grandchildren, singing, as he
goes, the song of the pasque flower, which he learned
as a child and which he now teaches to his grandchildren, commending to them the example of the
flower in its courage and endurance and faithfulness.

WORKS BY
MELVIN R. GILMORE[1]

Compiled by Alan R. Woolworth

"Exhibit of the Bureau of Plant Industry." *Cotner Collegian* 3 (Sept. 1904): 6–9.

"Origin of Easter Observances." *Cotner Collegian* 3 (Apr. 1905): 8–10.

"The Aboriginal Prohibition Law of Nebraska." *Cotner Collegian* 5 (Nov. 1906): 12–14.

"Indian Notes." In J. S. Morton and A. Watkins, eds., *Illustrated History of Nebraska* 2:221–22, 251–52, 254–55. Lincoln: J. North & Co., 1906.

"Sketch of a Trip among the Omahas." *Cotner Collegian* 4 (Mar. 1906): 7–9.

"Trip among the Omahas." *Cotner Collegian* 5 (Oct. 1906): 6–10.

With M. R. Blackman and R. F. Gilder. "Report of Museum Committee, Nebraska State Historical Society, February 1, 1907." *Nebraska Historical Publications* 15 (1907): 266–67.

"A Tribute to Wajapa." *Walthill* (Nebr.) *Times,* Aug. 30, 1907, p. 1.

"A Study in the Ethnobotany of the Omaha Indians." Master's thesis, University of Nebraska, 1909. Published in *Collections of the Nebraska State Historical Society* 17 (1913): 314–57.

---

[1]This bibliography, assembled over the last 30 years, includes Gilmore's published and unpublished works. While this is the most complete listing of Gilmore items known to the compiler, he wishes to acknowledge the helpful cross-check—and several additional items gleaned from—the bibliography of Gilmore's works compiled by David L. Erickson (see p. 219).

"The First Prohibition Law in America." *Journal of American History* 4 (July–Sept. 1910): 397–98.

"The Aboriginal Geography of the Nebraska Country." *Proceedings of the Mississippi Valley Historical Association* 6 (1913): 317–31.

"How Shall the Indian Be Treated Historically," by H. L. Keefe, with discussion by Melvin R. Gilmore. *Nebraska Historical Publications* 17 (1913): 277–84.

"Native Nebraska Shrubs Desirable for Decorative Planting." *44th Annual Report of the Nebraska State Horticultural Society* (1913): 248–49.

"Some Native Nebraska Plants with Their Uses by the Dakota." *Nebraska State Historical Society Collections* 17 (1913): 358–70.

"Site of Old Pawnee Village." 1 p. ms. with map, [1914?]. Gilmore Papers, Nebraska State Historical Society, Lincoln.

"Trip with White Eagle Determining Pawnee Sites, August 27-29." 7 p. ms., 1914. Gilmore Papers, Nebraska State Historical Society.

"Uses of Plants by the Indians of the Missouri River Region." Ph.D. diss., University of Nebraska, 1914. For published versions, see entries for 1919, below. The manuscript for vol. 2, "On the Ethnogeography of the Nebraska Region," is in Gilmore Papers, Nebraska State Historical Society.

"A Glimpse at Nebraska Indian Geography." *Journal of Geography* 13 (Feb. 1915): 179–85.

"University of Nebraska Campus Boulder." 4 p. ms., 1915. Gilmore Papers, Nebraska State Historical Society.

Toward the Sun. Poems by Aaron McGaffey Beede with commentary notes by Melvin R. Gilmore. Bismarck, N.Dak.: Bismarck Tribune Company, 1916.

"Primitive Agriculture—Indian Uses of Wild Plants." *The Word Carrier* 45 (Nov.–Dec. 1916): 24. Reprinted from the *Jamestown*

(N.Dak.) *Daily Alert;* first delivered as a speech at Cannonball, N.Dak.

"Ancient Indian Fireplaces in South Dakota Bad Lands: Fact and Fancy." *American Anthropologist* 19 (Oct.–Dec. 1917): 583–85.

"The Truth of the Wounded Knee Massacre." *American Indian Magazine* 5 (Oct.–Dec. 1917): 240–52.

"Indian Names of Melvin R. Gilmore." 2 p. ms., 1918. Gilmore Papers, Nebraska State Historical Society.

"Geographic Influences on Human Culture, with Special Reference to the Plains Region of North America." *Proceedings of the 22nd Annual Meeting of the North Dakota State Teachers Association* (Nov. 4–6, 1919): 87–93.

"The History of Corn." *Proceedings of the 22nd Annual Meeting of the North Dakota State Teachers Association* (Nov. 4–6, 1919): 93–100.

"The Mescal Society among the Omaha Indians." *Nebraska State Historical Society Publications* 19 (1919): 163–67.

"Some Indian Place Names in Nebraska." *Nebraska State Historical Society Publications* 19 (1919): 130–39.

"The True Logan Fontenelle." *Nebraska State Historical Society Publications* 19 (1919): 64–71.

"Uses of Plants by the Indians of the Missouri River Region." Bureau of American Ethnology, *Annual Report for 1911–12* 33 (1919): 43–154. Ph.D. diss., University of Nebraska, 1914. Published separately: Washington, D.C.: Government Printing Office, 1919; Lincoln: University of Nebraska, Bison Books, 1977.

"Food Stored by the Bean Mouse." *Journal of Mammalogy* 1 (1920): 157.

"List of Trees, Shrubs, Vines, Herbaceous Flowering Plants and Grasses Native to North Dakota and Suitable and Desirable for Use in Planting of Parks." *North Dakota Historical Collections* 6 (1920): 238–66.

"A Plea for Americanism." *The Word Carrier* 49 (Nov.–Dec. 1920): 22.

Review of *Minnesota Geographic Names: Their Origin and Historical Significance. Minnesota History Bulletin* 3 (Aug. 1920): 448–49.

"The Song of the Pasque Flower." *Dakota Farmer* (Aberdeen), May 15, 1920.

"State Historical Parks of North Dakota." *North Dakota Historical Collections* 6 (1920): 226–37.

"American Games for Girls." *Southern Workman* 50 (Nov. 1921): 510–12.

"Folklore Concerning the Meadow Lark." *Annals of Iowa* 13 (Apr. 1921): 137.

"The Ground Bean and the Bean Mouse and Their Economic Relations." *Annals of Iowa* 12 (Oct. 1921): 606–9.

"A Living Outdoor Museum." *Museum Work* 3 (Feb. 1921): 144–53.

"On the Name of the Woman Who Guided Lewis and Clarke [*sic*]." *Museum Work* 4 (July–Aug. 1921): 73–74.

Plant Relations in North Dakota. Extension Divison Bulletin no. 28, Educational Pamphlet Series no. 1. Grand Forks, N.Dak.: University of North Dakota, 1921.

The Song of the Pasque Flower: A Dakota Gift. Bismarck: Bismarck Tribune, 1921. 8 p. illustrated pamphlet.

"Use of the Ground Bean by Indians." *The Word Carrier* 50 (Jan.–Feb. 1921): 2–3.

"Meaning of the Word Dakota." *American Anthropologist* 24 (Jan.–Mar. 1922): 242–45.

"The Missouri River and the Indians." *North Dakota Good Roads Magazine* 2 (Aug. 15, 1922): 6–8.

"Some Comments on 'Aboriginal Tobaccos.' " *American Anthropologist* 24 (Oct.–Dec. 1922): 480–81.

"The Ground Bean." *Nebraska History* 6 (Oct.–Dec. 1923): 99–101.

"Arikara Fish-trap." *Indian Notes* 1 (July 1924): 120–34.

"Glass Bead Making by the Arikara." *Indian Notes* 1 (Jan. 1924): 20–21.

"Old Assiniboin Buffalo-drive in North Dakota." *Indian Notes* 1 (Oct. 1924): 204–11.

"Teokanha's Sacred Bundle." *Indian Notes* 1 (Apr. 1924): 52–62.

"Arikara Basketry." *Indian Notes* 2 (Apr. 1925): 89–95

"Arikara Household Shrine to Mother Corn." *Indian Notes* 2 (Jan. 1925): 31–34.

"Arikara Units of Measure." *Indian Notes* 2 (Jan. 1925): 64–66.

"Arikara Uses of Clay and of Other Earth Products." *Indian Notes* 2 (Oct. 1925): 283–89.

"The Ground Bean and Its Uses." *Indian Notes* 2 (July 1925): 178–87.

"Arikara Commerce." *Indian Notes* 3 (Jan. 1926): 13–18.

"Arikara Consolation Ceremony." *Indian Notes* 3 (Oct. 1926): 256–74.

"Arikara Genesis and Its Teachings." *Indian Notes* 3 (July 1926): 188–93.

"Buffalo-skull from the Arikara." *Indian Notes* 3 (Apr. 1926): 75–79.

"Some Cosmogonic Ideas of the Dakota." *American Anthropologist* 28 (July–Sept. 1926): 570–72.

"Dakota Mourning Customs." *Indian Notes* 3 (Oct. 1926): 295–96. From the texts of George Bushotter in the archives of the Bureau of American Ethnology.

"An Ethnobotanical Garden." *Southern Workman* 55 (May 1926): 220–23.

"The Game of Double-ball, or Twin-ball." *Indian Notes* 3 (Oct. 1926): 293–95.

"Being an Account of an Hidatsa Shrine and the Beliefs Respecting It." *American Anthropologist* 28 (July–Sept. 1926): 572–73.

"Indian Custom of 'Carrying the Pipe.'" *Indian Notes* 3 (Apr. 1926): 89–95.

"Indian Food Products from Native Wild Plants." *Good Health* 61 (Sept. 1926): 18–19, 46; (Oct. 1926) 12–13, 28.

"The Indian Garden." *Indian Notes* 3 (July 1926): 209–13.

"Preserve the Natural Beauty of America." *The National Plant, Flower, and Fruit Guild, Annual Report* 1926. New York. Reprinted as 6 p. pamphlet.

"Some Cosmogonic Ideas of the Dakota." *American Anthropologist* 28 (July–Sept. 1926): 570–72.

"Some Games of Arikara Children." *Indian Notes* 3 (Jan. 1926): 9–12.

"Some Indian Names." Letter to the editor of *Lincoln* (Nebr.) *State Journal,* Nov. 14, 1926, p. 4c.

"Some Interesting Indian Foods." *Good Health* 61 (July 1926): 12–14.

"Vegetable Foods of the American Indian." *Good Health* 61 (June 1926): 15–16, 22.

"The Coyote's Boxelder Knife." *Indian Notes* 4 (July 1927): 214–16.

"Dr. Gilmore's Field Researches in 1926." *Indian Notes* 4 (Apr. 1927): 166–69.

"Indians and Conservation of Native Life." *Torreya* 27 (Nov.–Dec. 1927): 97–98.

"Notes on Arikara Tribal Organization." *Indian Notes* 4 (Oct. 1927): 332–50.

"Oath-taking among the Dakota." Translation of text no. 240 of George Bushotter in the archives of the Bureau of American Ethnology. *Indian Notes* 4 (Jan. 1927): 81–83.

"Opportunities Offered by Native Plants." *Good Health* 62 (June 1927): 12–14.

"Origin of the Arikara Silverberry Drink." *Indian Notes* 4 (Apr. 1927): 125–27.

"The Missouri River and the Indians." Geographical Society of Philadelphia Bulletin no. 25 (Oct. 1927): 155–61.

"The Cattail Game of Arikara Children." *Indian Notes* 5 (July 1928): 316–18.

"In Aboriginal Days—Foods the Indians Prepared." *Good Health* 63 (Jan. 1928): 28–29.

"Indian Tribal Boundary-lines and Monuments." *Indian Notes* 5 (Jan. 1928): 59–63. Reprinted as "The Indian's Idea of Property Rights Was Misunderstood." *The American Indian* 2 (May 1928): 9.

"The Making of a New Head Chief by the Arikara." *Indian Notes* 5 (Oct. 1928): 411–18.

"Some Indian Ideas of Property." *Indian Notes* 5 (Apr. 1928): 137–44.

"Use of Cat-tails by Arikaras." *El Palacio* 24 (Feb. 1928): 114, 116.

"Arikara Account of the Origin of Tobacco and Catching of Eagles." *Indian Notes* 6 (Jan. 1929): 26–33. Reprinted in *The Word Carrier* 58 (Jan.–Feb. 1929): 4.

"The Dakota Ceremony of Hunká." *Indian Notes* 6 (Jan. 1929): 75–79.

"Greater Breeders Than Reid or Leaming." *Wallaces' Farmer* 54 (May 1929): 726, 734.

"A Mandan Monument to a National Hero." *Indian Notes* 6 (Apr. 1929): 147–51.

"Months and Seasons of the Arikara Calendar." *Indian Notes* 6 (July 1929): 246–50.

"The Old Time Method of Rearing a Dakota Boy." *Indian Notes* 6 (Oct. 1929): 367–71.

Prairie Smoke. Illustrated by Louis Schellbach. New York: Columbia University Press, 1929; St. Paul: Minnesota Historical Society Press, Borealis Books, 1987. Revised edition of *Prairie Smoke: A Collection of Lore of the Prairies.* Bismarck, N.Dak.: Bismarck Tribune Print, 1921; rev. ed., Bismarck, N.Dak.: Bismarck Tribune Print, 1922.

"The Arikara Book of Genesis." *Papers of the Michigan Academy of Science, Arts, and Letters* 12 (1929): 95–120.

"The Arikara Tribal Temple." *Papers of the Michigan Academy of Science, Arts, and Letters* 14 (1930): 47–70.

"Bluff Dwellers of the Ozarks." *El Palacio* 28 (1930): 182–84.

Indian Lore and Indian Gardens. Ithaca, N.Y.: Published under the auspices of the Coordinating Council on Nature Activities by the Slingerland-Comstock Company, 1930.

"Interesting Arikara Story of the Origin of the Tobacco." *The American Indian* 4 (Feb. 1930): 14.

"Keeper of the Arikara War Bundle Lived Righteous Life." *The American Indian* 4 (Apr. 1930): 6–7. Reprinted from "Notes on Arikara Tribal Organization," above (1927).

"Notes on Gynecology and Obstetrics of the Arikara Tribe of Indians." *Papers of the Michigan Academy of Science, Arts, and Letters* 14 (1930): 71–81.

"The Organization of the Ethnobotanical Laboratory." Paper read at the Anthropological Section of the American Association for the Advancement of Science, Cleveland, Dec. 1930. For published version, see *Ethnobotanical Laboratory,* below (1932).

"Vegetal Remains of the Ozark Bluff-Dweller Culture." *Papers of the Michigan Academy of Science, Arts, and Letters* 14 (1930): 83–102.

"Dispersal by Indians a Factor in the Extension of Discontinuous Distribution of Certain Species of Native Plants." *Papers of the Michigan Academy of Science, Arts, and Letters* 13 (1931): 89–94.

"Methods of Indian Buffalo Hunts, with the Itinerary of the Last Tribal Hunt of the Omaha." *Papers of the Michigan Academy of Science, Arts, and Letters* 16 (1931): 17–32.

Review of *The Forty-fifth and Forty-sixth Annual Reports of the Bureau of American Ethnology. Mississippi Valley Historical Review* 18 (June 1931): 74–76.

"The Sacred Bundles of the Arikara." *Papers of the Michigan Academy of Science, Arts, and Letters* 16 (1931): 33–50.

"Some Results of the First Year's Operation of the Ethnobotanical Laboratory." Paper read at the Anthropological Section of the American Association for the Advancement of Science, New Orleans, Dec. 1931. For published version, see *Ethnobotanical Laboratory,* below (1932).

"The Dakota Ceremony of Presenting a Pipe to Marshal Foch and Conferring a Name upon Him." *Papers of the Michigan Academy of Science, Arts, and Letters* 18 (1932): 15–21.

The Ethnobotanical Laboratory at the University of Michigan. Ann Arbor: University of Michigan Press, 1932. Contains reprints of articles published in the *American Anthropologist* 34 (Apr.–June 1932) and of papers delivered at the Anthropological Section of the American Association of the Advancement of Science, Cleveland, 1930, New Orleans, 1931.

"Importance of Ethnobotanical Investigation." *American Anthropologist* 34 (Apr.–June 1932): 320–27. Reprinted in *Ethnobotanical Laboratory,* above (1932).

"[Ethnobotanical] Methods." *American Anthropologist* 34 (Apr.–June 1932): 325–27. Reprinted in *Ethnobotanical Laboratory,* above (1932).

"Plant Vagrants in America." *Papers of the Michigan Academy of Science, Arts, and Letters* 15 (1932): 65–79.

"Prehistoric Man in Nebraska and the Great Plains Region: Western Plains Conference of Explorers, Lincoln, Nebr., 1932." Remarks by Gilmore and others. *Nebraska History* 13 (July–Sept. 1932): 163.

"Smoking among Aborigines." *El Palacio* 33 (Nov. 1932): 215–16.

"Some Chippewa Uses of Plants." *Papers of the Michigan Academy of Science, Arts, and Letters* 17 (1932): 119–43.

"The Victory Dance of the Dakota Indians at Fort Yates on the Standing Rock Reservation in November, 1918." *Papers of the Michigan Academy of Science, Arts, and Letters* 18 (1932): 23–30.

"Pasque Flower, Bloom of Dakota Folklore." *Nature* 21 (Jan. 1933): 17.

Review of *The Fighting Norths and Pawnee Scouts. North Dakota Historical Quarterly* 7 (Jan.–Apr. 1933): 172–73.

"The Arikara Method of Preparing a Dog for a Feast." *Papers of the Michigan Academy of Science, Arts, and Letters* 19 (1933): 37–38.

With E. R. Harlan, George Young Bear, and James Poweshiek. "An Original Study of Mesquakie (Fox) Life." *Annals of Iowa* 19 (Oct. 1933): 115–25, (Jan. 1934): 221–34, and (July 1934): 352–62; 20 (Oct. 1935): 123–39, and (Jan. 1937): 510–26.

"The Plight of Living Scalped Indians." *Papers of the Michigan Academy of Science, Arts, and Letters* 19 (1933): 39–45.

"An Interesting Vegetal Artifact from the Pecos Region of Texas." University of Texas Bulletin no. 3734, Anthropological Papers vol. 1 no. 5 (Sept. 1937): 17–26.

"An Arikara Bundle." *Indian Notes* 8 (Summer 1972): 93–98.

"Arikara Order of Butchering a Buffalo." *Indian Notes* 9 (Winter 1973): 21.

"Indian Agriculture in Nebraska." 5 p. ms., n.d. Gilmore Papers, Nebraska State Historical Society.

"The Legend of Pahuk." 7 p. ms., n.d. Gilmore Papers, Nebraska State Historical Society.

"Maize." 13 p. ms., n.d. Gilmore Papers, Nebraska State Historical Society.

"Notes on the Tribal Geography of the Dakotas." 10 p. ms., n.d. Gilmore Papers, Nebraska State Historical Society.

"The Presbyterian Mission to the Omahas." 2 p. ms., n.d. Gilmore Papers, Nebraska State Historical Society.

"A Proposition to Make a Survey of the Plant Lore and Geographic Lore of the Indian Tribes of Nebraska." 2 p. ms., n.d. Gilmore Papers, Nebraska State Historical Society.

"Some Food and Methods of Their Preparation among the Omaha Indians Previous to Their Europeanization." 3 p. ms., n.d. Gilmore Papers, Nebraska State Historical Society.

"Some Notes on Native Animals Known to the Omaha Indians." 20 p. ms., n.d. Gilmore Papers, Nebraska State Historical Society.

"Some Notes on the Indian Geography of Nebraska (with Special Reference to the Omahas)." 6 p. ms., n.d. Gilmore Papers, Nebraska State Historical Society.

"Wild Rice: A Most Excellent Native Grain." 3 p. ms., n.d. Gilmore Papers, Nebraska State Historical Society.

WORKS ABOUT
MELVIN R. GILMORE

Babcock, Willoughby M. Review of *Prairie Smoke*. *Mississippi Valley Historical Review* 16 (Sept. 1929): 273–74.

Erickson, David L. "Melvin Randolph Gilmore, Incipient Cultural Ecologist: A Biographic Analysis." Master's thesis, University of Nebraska, 1971. 137 p.

"Gilmore, Melvin Randolph." *Who Was Who in America, 1897–1942*, 458. Chicago: A. N. Marquis Co., 1942.

Jones, Volney H. Obituary of Melvin R. Gilmore. *Chronica Botanica* 6 (1941): 381–82.

Kroeber, A. L. Review of *Uses of Plants by Indians of the Missouri River Region*. *American Anthropologist* 22 (Oct.–Dec. 1920): 384–85.

"Melvin Gilmore, Ethnologist, 72." *New York Times*, July 27, 1940, p. 13.

Obituary of Melvin R. Gilmore. *New York Sun*, July 27, 1940, p. 15.

Stevens, O. A. Review of *Uses of Plants by the Indians of the Missouri River Region*. *Science* 52 (July 1920): 99–101.

Will, George F. "Dr. Melvin Randolph Gilmore." *North Dakota Historical Quarterly* 8 (Apr. 1941): 179–83.

INDEX

Aging, among Dakota, 136–38
Agriculture, xiv–xv, xxii, 83–84; irrigation, xv, 87; fields, 56; crops, 84–86, 87; tools, 87; property rights, 98–99. *See also* various crops
Arikara Indians, in Gilmore's studies, xxi; oral traditions, 10–13, 31–32, 123, 178–79, 185–88, 198–200; relations with other tribes, 10, 91; villages, 40, 185, 188; lodges, 56; agriculture, 86, 166–75, 178–79; described, 88–89; use of resources, 95; ceremonies, 173–74, 187–88, 200; migration, 184–85. *See also* Plains Indians
Ash, in pipestem, 106

Bad Water Village, Mandan, 131
Basket, magic, 63–67
Basswood, in earth lodge construction, 55
Bean mice, storehouses, 65–66; respected by Indians, 126–27, 194–95; in Omaha oral tradition, 127, 129–30; in Dakota oral tradition, 127–29; described, 194–95
Beans, cultivated, 84; traded, 89. *See also* Ground beans
Bearberry, in tobacco, 106
Beds, in tipis, 45, 59
Beloit, Kan., 18
Blackfoot, travels, 37–38
Blizzard, 116–18
Box elder, in Arikara tradition, 125

Brown thrasher, in Dakota tradition, 161
Buffalo, skull, 49; hides, 59, 90, 91; hunted, 96–97, 115–19, 162, 167–69, 175; in Mandan oral tradition, 119–20
Burial customs, Dakota Indians, 9–11

Caddoan group, described, 89; languages, 79
Cannonball River, N.Dak., 5
Catlinite, quarried, 97
Cedar (juniper), in oral tradition, 63, 180, 186–88; in ceremonies, 63, 180, 187–88
Central City, Nebr., 18
Ceremonies, Dakota, 48–50; Pawnee, 56–58; naming, 74–75; Arikara, 105–10; symbols in, 125–26; Sun Dance, 160; corn, 173–74
Cheyenne Indians, trade, 93
Chickadee, in oral tradition, 152–54
Children, care of, 43–45, 157; education, 45–47, 161–64, 190–91, 195; naming, 74; at play, 148–50, 163
Chippewa, relations with other tribes, 91–92; oral traditions, 195–98
Chokecherries, traded, 90–91
Christianity, among Indians, 126
Circle, sacred symbol, 52–54
Clark, William, nickname, 75–76
Clothing, Dakota, 44–45, 50
Corn (maize), cultivated, xxii, 84–86, 166, 171–72, 175–79;